Tibetan *vajras*
representing
thunderbolts
of the gods

Eyewitness
MYTHOLOGY

Written by
NEIL PHILIP

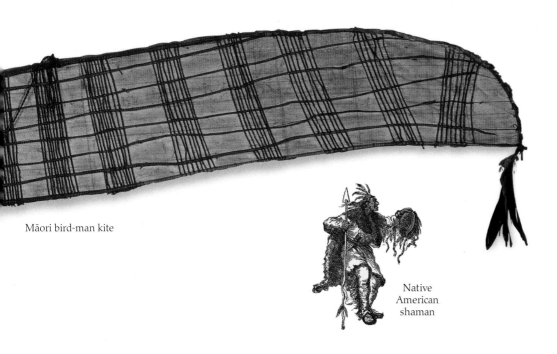

Māori bird-man kite

Native
American
shaman

Japanese
prayer
offerings

African fortune-telling
cowrie shells

Tangaroa, supreme god of Polynesia

Oceanic
ceremonial
axe

DK

LONDON, NEW YORK,
MELBOURNE, MUNICH, and DELHI

Project editor Melanie Halton
Art editor Joanne Connor
Senior managing editor Linda Martin
Senior managing art editor Julia Harris
Production Kate Oliver
Picture research Andy Sansom
DTP designer Andrew O'Brien

THIS EDITION
Editors Clare Hibbert, Steve Setford, Jessamy Wood
Art editors Rebecca Johns, Peter Radcliffe
Senior editor Shalia Awan
Managing editors Linda Esposito, Julie Ferris, Jane Yorke
Managing art editors Owen Peyton Jones, Jane Thomas
Art directors Simon Webb, Martin Wilson
Associate publisher Andrew Macintyre
Picture researchers Carolyn Clerkin, Harriet Mills
Production editors Jenny Jacoby, Hitesh Patel, Marc Staples
DTP designer Siu Yin Ho
Jacket editor Adam Powley
Editorial consultant Neil Philip

This Eyewitness ® Guide has been conceived by
Dorling Kindersley Limited and Editions Gallimard

First published in Great Britain in 1999.
This revised edition published in Great Britain in 2011 by
Dorling Kindersley Limited,
80 Strand, London WC2R ORL

Copyright © 1999, 2004, 2011 Dorling Kindersley Limited, London
A Penguin Company

2 4 6 8 10 9 7 5 3 1

175432 – 01/11

A CIP catalogue record for this book is
available from the British Library.

ISBN 978-1-40534-547-7

Colour reproduction by Colourscan,
Singapore; MDP, UK

Printed and bound by Toppan Printing Co.
(Shenzhen) Ltd, China

Discover more at
www.dk.com

Staff representing
African thunder
god Shango's axe

Back of Tangaroa

Eyewitness
MYTHOLOGY

Māori
ceremonial
adze (axe)

Monstrous
Chimera of
ancient
Greek
mythology

Ritual sword used
in Ogun worship,
west Africa

Medusa,
a hideous
Greek
gorgon

The Wealthy One
(1988), a contemporary
Native American mask

Hindu animal
god Garuda

Mould and casting of Venus,
Roman goddess of love

Contents

Native
American
Navajo
sand-painting

Native American
sand-painting
pigments

What is mythology?

MOTHER EARTH
This gold pendant shows Astarte, the Canaanite goddess of fertility. A great mother goddess appears in most mythologies. The Egyptian goddess Isis speaks for all: "I am Nature, the universal Mother."

THE WORD "MYTH" comes from the Greek *mythos*, meaning a word or a story. In everyday speech it often refers to something people believe that is not really true: "It's a myth that carrots help you see in the dark." But mythology is not a collection of lies; it is a collection of stories that help people to make sense of the world. Each human culture makes stories about the creation of Earth, the origins of humankind, and the meaning of life. Mythology puts across religious ideas in the form of stories. But while the essence of religious belief is usually very simple, mythology can be highly complex. This is because myths are stories that explore rather than explain. They show the human mind searching to balance the forces of creation and destruction, of life and death.

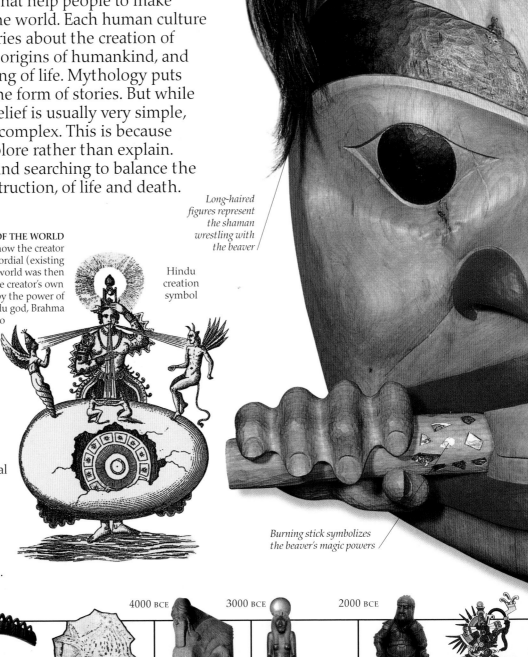

Long-haired figures represent the shaman wrestling with the beaver

CREATION OF THE WORLD
Numerous mythologies tell how the creator emerged from a cosmic egg or a primordial (existing from the beginning) ocean. The world was then brought into being, perhaps from the creator's own body, perhaps from mud, or even by the power of words or thought. The first Hindu god, Brahma (pp.14, 50, 56), is sometimes said to have been born from a golden egg that floated on the first waters.

Hindu creation symbol

Myth beginnings

Humankind has made myths from the dawn of history. The oldest living mythology is that of the Australian Aborigines, whose stories of the sacred eternal Dreamtime, or Dreaming, stretch back 40,000 years. The myths of diverse cultures are often linked by similar themes. This timeline shows the approximate dates that individual societies began recording or shaping their myths.

Burning stick symbolizes the beaver's magic powers

40000 BCE	10000 BCE		4000 BCE	3000 BCE		2000 BCE	
Aboriginal Dreamtime tools	African god Eshu	Siberian Chukchi world on a sealskin	Sumerian winged bull	Egyptian cat god Sekhmet		Chinese war god Guan Di	Mesoamerican god Quetzalcoatl

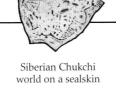
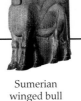

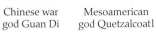

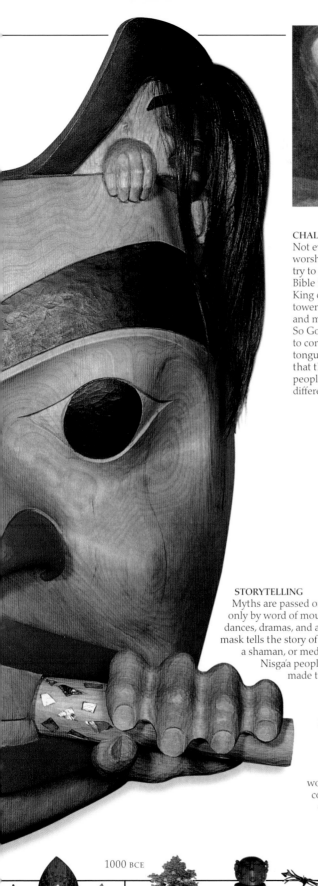

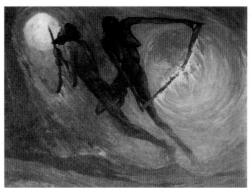

GUIDING ANCESTORS
Ancestors play an important role in world mythology. For Australian Aborigines, the laws and customs established by ancestor spirits (left) act as guidelines for life today. These ancestors exist outside of time, in the eternal present of the Dreamtime. Aboriginal myths are stories of the Dreamtime, and Aboriginal art and ceremonies are ways of connecting with the ancestors.

CHALLENGING THE GODS
Not everyone is content to worship the gods; some people try to challenge them. The Bible tells how Nimrod, King of Babylon, built a tower to reach heaven and make war on God. So God sent 70 angels to confuse the builders' tongues. Some say that this is why people now speak different languages.

The Tower of Babel fell when the workmen could no longer understand one another

STORYTELLING
Myths are passed on by storytelling – stories told not only by word of mouth and in writing, but also in rituals, dances, dramas, and artworks. This Medicine Beaver mask tells the story of the life-or-death struggle between a shaman, or medicine man, of the North American Nisga'a people and a giant beaver. The shaman made the beaver into his spirit helper.

PERSEPHONE AND HADES
Many mythologies hope for a new life after death. The ancient Egyptians and Greeks both linked the idea of an afterlife with the annual death and resurrection of corn. The Greeks worshipped Persephone, daughter of the corn goddess Demeter (p.24), as Queen of the Dead, in rites that they believed held the entire human race together.

1000 BCE   1 CE   1000 CE

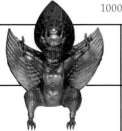
Hindu figure of Garuda

Bible story of Adam and Eve

Polynesian god Tangaroa

Greek supreme god Zeus

Celtic horned god Cernunnos

Roman war god Mars

Norse god Thor's hammer

Japanese prayer offering

Creation of the world

COSMIC EGG
A bird-man from Rapa Nui (Easter Island, in the Pacific Ocean) is shown holding the cosmic egg that contains the world. In the nesting season, the man whose servant was the first to gather an egg became Rapa Nui's Bird-Man, the living representative for that year of the creator god Makemake.

MANY PEOPLES SEEM TO AGREE that the world was made as a deliberate act of creation by a divine being. Often the world is described as having originally been all ocean, and it is from the sea that the world emerges in the earliest myths. Nun was the god of the ancient Egyptian mythological ocean. The Arctic Tikigaq people say that Raven made the land by harpooning a great whale, which then floated and became dry land. Sometimes there are two creators, who together shape the world. For example, First Creator and Lone Man (p.18) of the Native American Mandan tribe sent a mud hen to Earth to fetch mud from the bottom of the flood waters to make the first land.

FIRE AND ICE
The Vikings believed that the world began when fire from the south met ice from the north. At the centre, the ice began to thaw. As it dripped, it shaped itself into the first being, Ymir, whose sweat formed the first frost giants. Then the ice-melt shaped a cow, whose milk fed Ymir. As the cow licked the ice, she shaped the first man, Buri.

Pottery figurine of Gaia from Thebes, 450 BCE

FLOATING DISC
According to the ancient Greeks, the first to be born from the primeval, or original, chaos was Gaia, or Earth. Gaia was conceived as a disc floating on a waste of waters, and encircled by the river Oceanus. Gaia gave birth to Uranus (the sky) and Cronos (time).

Ahura Mazda

THE BIG BANG
Scientists now believe the world began with the Big Bang, a huge explosion 13,000 million years ago that sent matter in all directions to create the ever-expanding Universe.

CREATED FROM GOODNESS
The ancient Persians believed in twin spirits who had existed since the beginning of time: Ahura Mazda, who was good, and Ahriman, who was evil. It was Ahura Mazda who created the physical world, set time in motion, and created humankind.

Part of the ancient Persian Tree of Life relief, 9th century BCE

TURTLE ISLAND
According to the mythologies of many Native American tribes, the world is supported on a turtle's back. The Seneca tribe believed that when the first woman fell down from another world in the sky, the toad that lived on the primal waters dived down to fetch mud to place on the turtle's back. The mud, which became Earth, provided support for the first woman.

The first land was said to have been created on a turtle's back

19th-century Native American Cheyenne shield

The Milky Way and the planets of the Solar System

CURDLING OCEAN
The Japanese god Izanagi (pp.21, 31) and his wife Izanami stood on the Floating Bridge of Heaven and stirred the ocean with a jewelled spear until it curdled and formed the first island, Onokoro. They built a house there, with a central stone pillar that is the backbone of the world.

Vishnu sits on top of Mount Mandara

OCEAN CHURNING
At the beginning of this cycle of creation, a number of vital treasures, including the elixir of immortality, were not to be found, so the Hindu gods decided to churn the ocean, using Mount Mandara as the paddle. As they churned, the ocean turned first to milk, then to butter, and then the Sun and Moon arose. As they churned some more, the elixir was finally created.

Vasuki, the cosmic serpent, was used as a rope to twist the mountain

The mountain is supported by a giant turtle

The cosmos

PEOPLE HAVE ALWAYS QUESTIONED the mysteries of the world, from its origin and shape to its cosmos, or order. The world is often thought to have emerged from a cosmic egg. In China, the warring forces of yin and yang in the egg created the first being, Pan Gu. The Dogon people of west Africa believe the world was formed from a vibrating egg that burst open to reveal a creator spirit. The Ainu of Japan believed there were six skies above this Earth, and six worlds below it – the abodes of gods, demons, and animals. The world has long been thought of as round. A myth told by the Inuit people of the Arctic tundra tells how two families set out in opposite directions to discover the size of the world. When they met up again, they were very old, but the fact that they came back to where they started proved that the world is round. The Mangaian people of Polynesia say that the Universe is held in the shell of a huge coconut.

Inuit people of the Arctic tundra build igloos, which are round like the world

WORLD IN A SEALSKIN
On this sealskin painted by the Chukchi people of Siberia, the whole Arctic world – Sun, Moon, land, sea, and sky – is captured in a small space. Human beings share creation with spirits, animals, and gods such as the creator Raven and his wife Miti, and Sedna (p.23), the mother of the sea beasts.

YIN AND YANG
The ancient Chinese believed that the first being, Pan Gu, was created inside a cosmic egg by the opposing forces of yin and yang. When at last the conflict between yin and yang broke the egg open, Pan Gu was born, and he pushed the sky away from Earth. After he died, exhausted by this labour, his body formed the mountains and the land –

Yin and yang symbolize universal opposites, such as good and evil, that must be equally balanced for a harmonious world

Brahma, the creator of the Universe, is shown on Vishnu's forehead

Vishnu's conch shell symbolizes the very first vibration of the Universe – the sound "om"

The discus symbolizes the mind and the Sun

WORLD TREE
The Vikings, or Norsemen, of Scandinavia believed there were nine worlds, including humankind's Middle Earth. These worlds were arranged in three layers around Yggdrasil, a huge ash tree at the centre of the cosmos. The worlds of gods, giants, elves, dwarfs, humans, and the dead were all sustained by Yggdrasil, the World Tree.

COSMIC STONE

This Babylonian boundary stone shows the gods and goddesses of the Babylonian cosmos as witnesses to a legal agreement. At the top are symbols of the goddess of love and war, Ishtar (p.25); the Moon god, Sin; and the Sun god, Shamash (p.13). An underworld snake wriggles up the side. The scorpion in the centre row is the symbol of Ishhara – the goddess of marriage and childbirth, and the enforcer of oaths.

Sin, the Moon god, is represented by a crescent Moon

This symbol for the planet Venus represents Ishtar, the goddess of love and war

Vishnu's lotus flower is a symbol of purity

NUT AND GEB

The ancient Egyptians thought that Earth was male, personified by Geb, the Earth god. Geb mated with his sister Nut, the sky goddess, to produce the stars. Nut and Geb were wrenched apart by their father Shu, god of the air, who holds Nut aloft and pins Geb down with his feet.

Each night the Sun god Ra is swallowed by Nut, to be born again the next morning

Underworld snakes writhe in the lowest region of the cosmos, Tala, where murderers are reborn

This golden mace is a symbol of knowledge

Watchful eyes of the owl Koururu, sacrificed by Rongo, god of agriculture, to protect his house

Varuna, god of the waters, sits on an imaginary beast

This carving stood at the entrance to a Māori assembly house on North Island, New Zealand

PAPA AND RANGI

The Māori of New Zealand tell how Papa, the Earth goddess, coupled with Rangi, the sky god. So closely did Papa and Rangi cling to each other that their children could not leave the Earth womb. Eventually, Papa and Rangi were forced apart by one of their children, Tane (pp.23, 34), the forest god.

VISHNU'S WORLD

Vishnu, the Preserver (pp.18, 26), is one of the three great gods of the Hindu religion. At the end of each cycle of creation, Vishnu sleeps on the world serpent Shesha, preserving the seed of a new creation that will rise when he wakes. When Vishnu was incarnated as the hero Krishna (p.32), his mother looked into his mouth and saw the whole Universe. This 19th-century painting shows Vishnu as the Universe.

Sun and Moon

THE SUN AND THE MOON, which light up the sky by day and at night and enable us to tell the time, have been the subjects of many myths. For the Native American Zuni people, Moonlight-Giving Mother and Sun Father are the givers of light and life. The Native American Cherokee say the Sun is female, and tell of her grief when her daughter died from a rattlesnake bite. Sun hid herself away, the world grew dark, and her tears caused a flood. Only the dancing and singing of young men and women could cheer her up. The Arctic Chukchi tell how a woman married the Sun, but a black beetle took her place. It was only when her son sought out his father that the imposter was discovered. Another Chukchi woman married the Moon. She had been deserted by her husband and left to starve, but she crawled to Moon's house and became his wife.

DEALER OF DAYS
The Moon god Thoth was in charge of the ancient Egyptian calendar, which had 12 months of 30 days each. The sky goddess Nut (p.11), who had been cursed never to give birth, won five extra days from Thoth in which she had her children.

ROMAN GODDESS DIANA
Diana (p.35), Artemis in Greek mythology, is shown here with her foot resting on the Moon, with which she was closely associated. More often, however, she is depicted with a crescent Moon in her hair.

The goddess Diana, with one foot on the Moon

The face on this Inuit mask represents the spirit of the Moon

Decorative feathers represent the stars

The white border around the face symbolizes the air

Native American Haida mask

Painted Moon face sculpted in wood

FEEDING HUMANKIND
The Inuit people of the Arctic have a Moon Man called Igaluk or Tarqeq. Shamans (medicine men) make spirit journeys to ask him to ensure that he will send animals for men to hunt. Moon Man also helps the souls of the dead to be reborn as humans, animals, or fish.

POLLUTING THE WORLD
A Native American Haida myth tells how Wultcixaiya, the son of the Moon, rescued his sister from her unhappy marriage to Pestilence. Wearing a steel coat, he broke into Pestilence's house of rock, freeing his sister, but also polluting the world with sickness and disease.

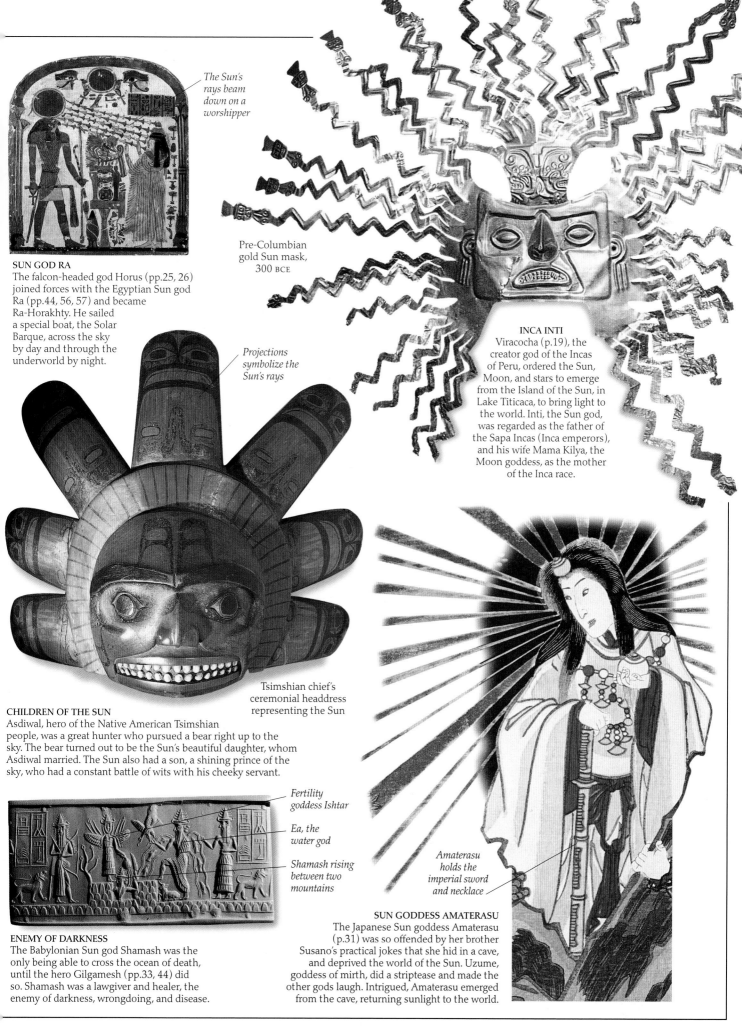

SUN GOD RA
The falcon-headed god Horus (pp.25, 26) joined forces with the Egyptian Sun god Ra (pp.44, 56, 57) and became Ra-Horakhty. He sailed a special boat, the Solar Barque, across the sky by day and through the underworld by night.

The Sun's rays beam down on a worshipper

Pre-Columbian gold Sun mask, 300 BCE

INCA INTI
Viracocha (p.19), the creator god of the Incas of Peru, ordered the Sun, Moon, and stars to emerge from the Island of the Sun, in Lake Titicaca, to bring light to the world. Inti, the Sun god, was regarded as the father of the Sapa Incas (Inca emperors), and his wife Mama Kilya, the Moon goddess, as the mother of the Inca race.

Projections symbolize the Sun's rays

Tsimshian chief's ceremonial headdress representing the Sun

CHILDREN OF THE SUN
Asdiwal, hero of the Native American Tsimshian people, was a great hunter who pursued a bear right up to the sky. The bear turned out to be the Sun's beautiful daughter, whom Asdiwal married. The Sun also had a son, a shining prince of the sky, who had a constant battle of wits with his cheeky servant.

Fertility goddess Ishtar

Ea, the water god

Shamash rising between two mountains

Amaterasu holds the imperial sword and necklace

ENEMY OF DARKNESS
The Babylonian Sun god Shamash was the only being able to cross the ocean of death, until the hero Gilgamesh (pp.33, 44) did so. Shamash was a lawgiver and healer, the enemy of darkness, wrongdoing, and disease.

SUN GODDESS AMATERASU
The Japanese Sun goddess Amaterasu (p.31) was so offended by her brother Susano's practical jokes that she hid in a cave, and deprived the world of the Sun. Uzume, goddess of mirth, did a striptease and made the other gods laugh. Intrigued, Amaterasu emerged from the cave, returning sunlight to the world.

Making humankind

SNAKE GODDESS
Nü Wa, the first Chinese goddess, had the face of a girl but the body of a snake. She was lonely, so she made the first human beings out of mud and water to cheer herself up.

ALL MYTHOLOGIES TELL how the first human beings were made. Often the creator shaped them from clay or mud. The Unalit (North Alaskan Inuit) say that the first man was born from the pod of a beach pea. When he burst out of the pod, he was met by Raven, who taught him how to live and made him a wife out of clay. The ancient Egyptians believed that the first human beings were made from the tears of Ra (pp.13, 44, 56, 57), the Sun god. For the Serbians, people were made from the creator's sweat, which is why they say we are doomed to a life of toil. The Norse god Odin (p.37) made the first man and woman from driftwood, but there is also a myth telling how the Norse god Heimdall fathered the various kinds of men: serfs, warriors, and kings.

Brahma has four heads so that he can see in all directions

Tangaroa brings forth other beings

BRAHMA THE CREATOR
The Hindu creator Brahma (pp. 6, 50, 56) is the universal soul, the Self-Existent Great-Grandfather. He made the world and everything in it. He is sometimes called Purusha, the First Being. As Purusha, he divided himself into two, male and female, and mated in the form of every creature, from humans to ants.

Carved wooden bowl from the Yoruba in west Africa

The cosmic serpent Aido-Hwedo coiled itself around Earth

BODIES OF CLAY
The west African creator Mawu-Lisa (pp.16, 36) made the first people from clay and water. The first man and woman, sometimes called Adanhu and Yewa, were sent down from the sky with the Rainbow Snake Aido-Hwedo (pp.50, 56). For the first 17 days it did nothing but rain. The man and woman did not speak to each other, but only called out the name of the god who had sent them to Earth.

Adanhu

Yewa

Wooden statue from the Tubuaï Islands in Polynesia, where the supreme god Tangaroa is called A'a

Wooden idols

FIRST HUMANS
When the statue of Tangaroa (left) was first discovered, it contained wooden idols like those above, which represented the first men and women.

New beings crawl on Tangaroa's back

POTTER'S PEOPLE
The Egyptian ram-god Khnum was the potter who shaped each human being and his or her *ka*, or life force, on his potter's wheel. He was worshipped at the island of Elephantine with his wife Satet and their daughter Anuket, the huntress. An inscription on a block of granite found at Elephantine records how prayers to Khnum brought to an end a seven-year famine.

Tangaroa's body cavity contained wooden idols

The tree of the knowledge of good and evil

WOODEN STATUES
Tangaroa (p.34) is the Polynesian god of the ocean. In some places he is considered the maker of all things. In Tahiti it is said that Tangaroa lived inside the cosmic egg at the beginning of time. When he broke out, he called, "Who's there?" There was no reply, so Tangaroa created the world, and called forth gods and humans from his body.

Tangaroa creates other gods and humankind from his body

ADAM AND EVE
According to the Bible, God created Adam, the first man, in his own image. God shaped Adam out of clay and made him a companion, Eve, the first woman, from one of Adam's ribs. Islamic tradition says that when God, Allah in Arabic, breathed life into Adam's nostrils, Adam sneezed and said, "Praise be to Allah."

15

Supreme beings

ONE GOD who reigns over all others is part of most mythologies. These supreme gods may be associated with the creation of the world and humankind. Many supreme deities, such as the Greek god Zeus, are essentially sky gods; others may be Sun, battle, city, or tribal gods. In some cultures, especially in Africa, the supreme god is thought to have retired from the world after the initial creation. This is the case with Nana-Buluku, the creator deity of the Fon people of west Africa, and with Nyame of the west African Ashanti people. Over time, such gods are sometimes almost forgotten. For example, Nana-Buluku's daughter Mawu-Lisa (pp.14, 36) is now routinely described as the creator, and the word *mawu* has come to mean "god" in the Fon language.

Thunderbolts were made for Zeus by the cyclopes, giants who helped in the war against Cronos, Zeus's father

RULER OF THE GREEKS
Zeus (known as Jupiter to the Romans) was the ruler of the Greek gods. Zeus overthrew his father, Cronos, before establishing his rule on Mount Olympus. His wife Hera, the goddess of marriage, was jealous because of his many love affairs, during which he fathered the gods Apollo and Artemis, and the heroes Perseus (p.33) and Heracles (p.26).

Made of bronze and decorated with silver, this late Bronze-Age figure represents the storm god Baal

THE RAINMAKER
The Canaanite storm god Baal made thunder with his mace and produced lightning from his lance. Baal revolted against El, his father, by defeating El's favourite, Yam, the god of the sea. Another myth tells of his long battle against Mot, the god of death.

BABYLONIAN KING OF THE GODS
This dog-like dragon is the symbol of Marduk, the Babylonian king of the gods. Strong and heroic, he was given authority over the other gods, including his father, Ea, the god of wisdom, when he agreed to slay the dragon Tiamat (one of two primal beings). Marduk created humankind from the blood of Kingu, Tiamat's son.

FEATHERED SERPENT
Half snake, half quetzal bird, Quetzalcoatl was the Aztec lord of life and god of the winds. He descended to the underworld to retrieve the bones of early humans in order to create new beings. The underworld was ruled by his father, the death god Mictlantecuhtli (p.53).

The feathers of more than 250 quetzal birds make up this headdress

Aztec serpent god Quetzalcoatl

Quetzal headdress of Montezuma II, the last Aztec ruler

Wooden *kantele* from Karelia in Finland, 1893

Stoneware Taoist shrine of the Ming dynasty, 1406 CE

Lao-tzu, the founder of Taoism, is shown riding a buffalo

SINGING SHAMAN

Väinämöinen, the eternal singer, was the son of the Finnish air goddess Ilmatar. He was born old, so no one wanted to marry him. One girl, Aino, even preferred to become a mermaid rather than be his bride. Väinämöinen was a shaman (spiritual guide) whose songs to the sound of his harp-like *kantele* were acts of creative magic.

The Jade Emperor

LORD OF THE HEAVENS

The Chinese gods formed a huge bureaucracy, at the head of which was the Jade Emperor. He was assisted by the God of the Eastern Peak, who had no fewer than 75 departments under his control, each supervised by lesser gods. The Jade Emperor's wife was Xi Wang Mu, the Queen Mother of the West and the guardian of the peaches of immortality, which she served at a great feast once every 1,000 years.

Ebony pestle and mortar from Tanzania, east Africa

Mortar

Pestle

The God of the Eastern Peak

STAIRWAY TO HEAVEN

Nyame is the sky god of the Ashanti of Africa. He used to live close to humans, but when an old woman annoyed him by knocking him with her pestle as she pounded yams, he moved away towards the heavens. The old woman and her sons tried to reach him by piling mortars on top of one another, but they were one short. They took the mortar from the bottom to place it on the top, but the pile collapsed, killing them all.

Floods and storms

THE STORY OF A GREAT FLOOD that once overwhelmed the world – a flood that only a lucky few survived – is one of the most widespread of all myths. The earliest flood story is found in the Mesopotamian *Epic of Gilgamesh*, in which Utnapishtim frees birds to see if the waters are subsiding. The Native American Mandan tribe told of Lone Man (p.8), who survived a great flood in his Big Canoe. The Greek god Zeus (p.16), tired of the wickedness of humans, sent a flood to drown them all. But the giant Prometheus warned his son Deucalion, who built an ark in time to save himself and his wife.

SAVED BY A FISH
One day the Hindu wise man Manu found a fish in his washing water. The fish told Manu that he should build a ship because a great flood was coming. When the flood arrived, the fish, which was really an incarnation of the Hindu god Vishnu (pp.11, 26, 32), towed Manu to safety. Manu then became the father of all humankind.

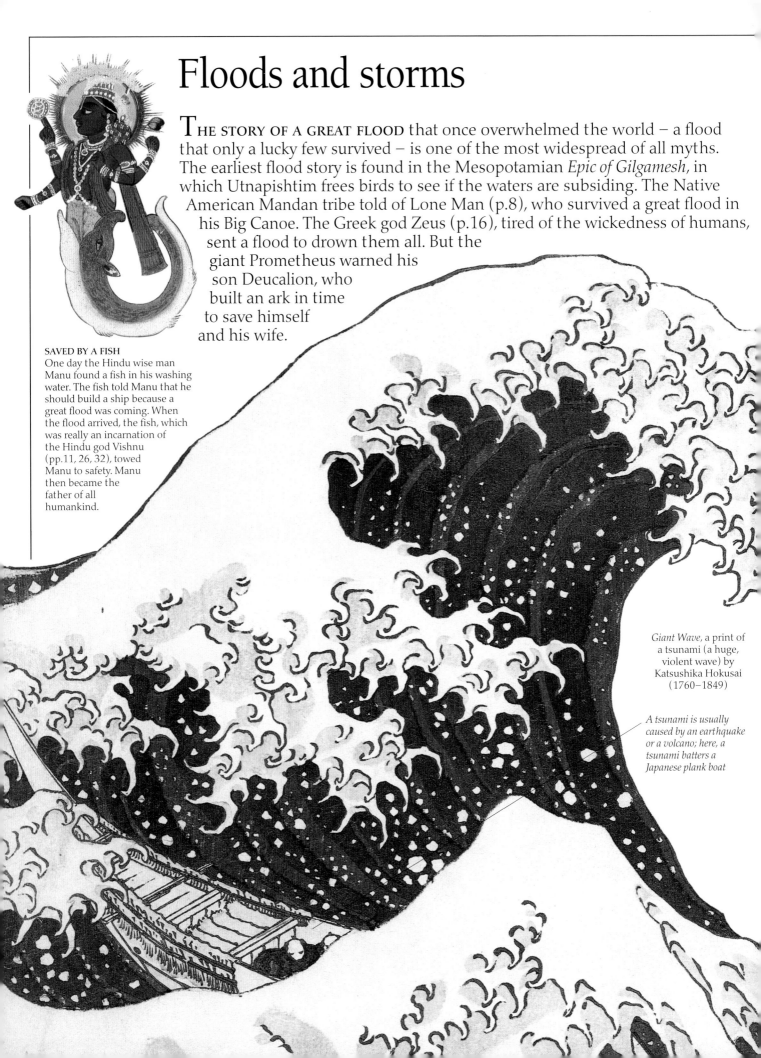

Giant Wave, a print of a tsunami (a huge, violent wave) by Katsushika Hokusai (1760–1849)

A tsunami is usually caused by an earthquake or a volcano; here, a tsunami batters a Japanese plank boat

KINGDOM OF ATLANTIS

Poseidon (p.21), the Greek god of the sea, fell in love with a woman called Cleito, and built her a paradise island. The sons that Cleito bore Poseidon founded the kingdom of Atlantis on the island. The brothers ruled the island together in wisdom. But later rulers became greedy and corrupt, so Poseidon sent a tidal wave to swallow up Atlantis and all of its people.

MAYAN RAINMAKER

Chac, the Mayan rain god, broke open a great rock to uncover the first maize plant. And it was Chac who sent the rain each year to enable the maize to grow. But sometimes, instead of gentle rain, Chac sent violent storms, in which he wielded his weapon of lightning.

Headdress of tropical bird feathers

Type of poncho (blanket-like cloak) worn by the Sapa Incas – the rulers of the Inca empire

In his left hand, Chac carries a bowl; in his right is a ball of smoking incense

GIANT WAVES

The great flood is caused either by a deluge of rain, as in the Noah story (below), or by a gigantic tidal wave that sweeps over the land, as in the story of Atlantis (above). Both are terrifying images of unstoppable destruction.

CREATOR OF HUMANS

Viracocha (p.13), the Inca creator god, was displeased with his first attempt at creating humans from stone, so he drowned them all in a flood. He then tried again, this time making the people from clay. He wandered among these new people as a beggar, teaching them how to live. The first Sapa Inca (Inca emperor) named himself after Viracocha.

NOAH AND THE ARK

When God saw how wicked humans had become, he decided to drown them all, for he was sorry he had ever created them. But he decided to save one good man, Noah. He warned Noah to build an ark in which to save his family and two of every living creature in order to repopulate the Earth after the great flood. When the flooding subsided, God set a rainbow in the sky as a promise that he would never again destroy humanity with a flood.

Some believe that gods live at the peak of Mount Fuji in Japan, which is nearly always capped with snow

The elements

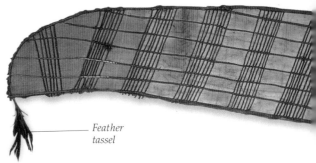

Feather
tassel

ALL OVER THE WORLD, the elemental forces that shape our planet have been the focus of myth-making. Fire, air, earth, and water are known as the four elements in Western tradition. The Chinese have five elements: wood, fire, earth, metal, and water. Almost all mythologies tell how humans acquired the gift of fire, often stolen from the Sun. Gods of the air and the sky have been so important that the names of many supreme gods, such as the Greek god Zeus, simply mean "sky". Earth, though sometimes regarded as male, is more often thought of as our mother. According to the mythology of ancient Babylon, in the beginning nothing existed but Apsu, the freshwater ocean, and Tiamat, the saltwater ocean. These two waters have given and taken life since the dawn of time.

Pele,
Hawaiian
goddess
of fire

*Agni's stomach
is full because fire
devours everything*

Olokun, sea
king of the Edo
people of Benin,
Nigeria

FIRE-EATER
Wherever a fire is lit, the Hindu fire god Agni is born. Because he is present in all homes, he knows all secrets. He once helped a man find his wife, who had been carried away by the wise man Bhrigu. Bhrigu then cursed Agni, making him consume all the dirt of the Earth. But as Agni devours the dirt, he also purifies it with his flames.

VOLCANIC PELE
In Hawaii, which is dominated by the Kilauea volcano, Pele is worshipped as the goddess of fire. She is as passionate and dangerous as a volcano. Pele fell in love with the prince of Kauai, but when he preferred her sister, she encased him in molten lava and turned him to stone.

OCEANS OF OLOKUN
Olokun, the sea king of the Edo people of Benin, Nigeria, is a powerful god. He is the source of all wealth and the bringer of children, whose souls must cross the ocean to be born. His palace is a paradise, full of the noise of children and his wives, who are the rivers. The Olokun River is the source of all the waters of Earth, including the ocean.

Mother-of-pearl eyes embedded in a painted face

Kite is made of canvas and twigs

SKY MAN
Tawhaki, the great Polynesian hero whom New Zealand's Māoris regard as the god of thunder and lightning, ascended to the sky world as a kite, seeking to avenge his father, Hema, whose eyes had been gouged out by goblins to use as lights. Māori priests foretold the future by watching the dance of kites in the air.

Māori kite in the form of a bird with a human head

Balls of rolling thunder

The thunder god is depicted as a demon in the air

Drumstick makes thunder

EARTH MOTHER
Toci, mother of the gods, was an important Aztec Earth goddess. She was a goddess of the harvest, childbirth, and curing, but also of war and discord. Earth itself was said to have been made by the gods from the body of the fearsome goddess Tlaltecuhtli, who could be appeased only by being given human hearts to eat.

Aztec Earth-goddess statue (c.1300–1500 CE)

Poseidon's trident, a three-pronged fisherman's spear

THUNDER ROLLS
This burly Japanese god (possibly Kami-Nari, the god of rolling thunder) beats out thunder on his drum. Japanese thunder deities are threatening forces. When the god Izanagi (pp.9, 31) descended to hell in search of his wife Izanami, she sent eight thunder gods to chase him from the underworld.

Aboriginal stone axe from Northern Territory, Australia

LIGHTNING MAN
Namarrgon, the Lightning Man of Australia's Northern Territory Aborigines, uses stone axes to split the dark clouds when he shakes the ground with thunder and lightning. He is capable of causing widespread devastation, and sometimes strikes and kills people at the request of sorcerers.

STORMY SEAS
Poseidon (pp.19, 26), the Greek god of the sea, was violent and vengeful. He showed this in his persecution of Odysseus (p.27), who had blinded Poseidon's son. As well as making storms at sea, Poseidon was also thought to cause earthquakes.

Japanese thunder god

The natural world

ALL THE ELEMENTS OF THE NATURAL WORLD – animals, flowers, plants, and trees – are considered gifts of the gods, and they remain in their care. Many cultures worshipped Earth as a mother goddess, a provider of food and fertility. But they also gave responsibility for important crops – such as maize for Native Americans, or rice for the Japanese – to specific gods or goddesses. Hunting societies believe that game is withheld or released by the gods, such as Sedna, the North American Inuit mistress of the sea beasts. In the forests of northern Cameroon, hunters pray to the Bedimo (ancestral spirits) to release game from their divine stables.

This type of reed has been used to make pipes for 5,000 years

Spanish reed

Cobs of maize

PAN'S PIPES
With his goat-like horns and legs, Pan was the Greek god of the pastures, especially of sheep and goats. He could inspire fear in his enemies, who would flee in what we now call a panic. Pan was also very amorous. One nymph, Syrinx, turned into reeds to escape him. But Pan made himself a set of musical pipes from the reeds so that she would always be close to him.

SPRINGTIME GOD
The Aztec god of spring, Xipe Totec, allowed his skin to be flayed (peeled off) in order to promote new growth from within – like a maize seed breaking through its husk to become a new plant. At festivals in his honour, young men wore the skins of human sacrificial offerings.

Farmers harvesting rice

RICE SUPPLIES
Every village in Japan has a shrine dedicated to the rice god Inari, who comes down from his mountain home in the spring and returns in the autumn, after the rice harvest.

Rice grains

22

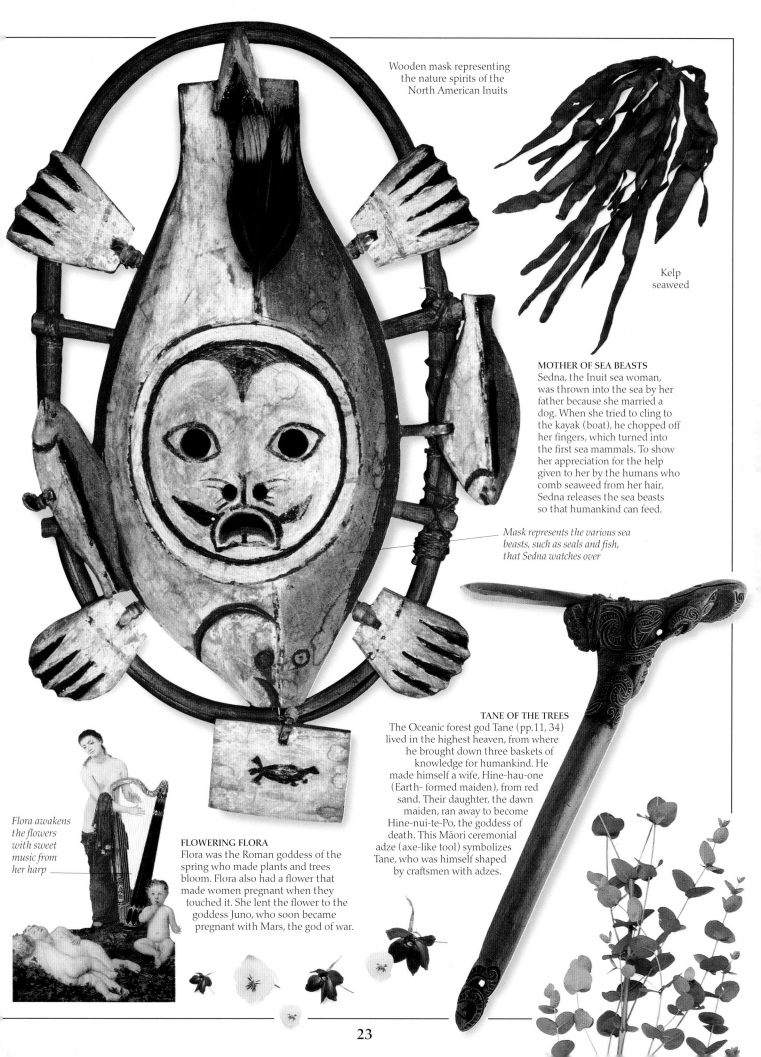

Wooden mask representing the nature spirits of the North American Inuits

Kelp seaweed

MOTHER OF SEA BEASTS
Sedna, the Inuit sea woman, was thrown into the sea by her father because she married a dog. When she tried to cling to the kayak (boat), he chopped off her fingers, which turned into the first sea mammals. To show her appreciation for the help given to her by the humans who comb seaweed from her hair, Sedna releases the sea beasts so that humankind can feed.

Mask represents the various sea beasts, such as seals and fish, that Sedna watches over

Flora awakens the flowers with sweet music from her harp

FLOWERING FLORA
Flora was the Roman goddess of the spring who made plants and trees bloom. Flora also had a flower that made women pregnant when they touched it. She lent the flower to the goddess Juno, who soon became pregnant with Mars, the god of war.

TANE OF THE TREES
The Oceanic forest god Tane (pp.11, 34) lived in the highest heaven, from where he brought down three baskets of knowledge for humankind. He made himself a wife, Hine-hau-one (Earth- formed maiden), from red sand. Their daughter, the dawn maiden, ran away to become Hine-nui-te-Po, the goddess of death. This Māori ceremonial adze (axe-like tool) symbolizes Tane, who was himself shaped by craftsmen with adzes.

Celtic bronze horse found in the tomb of a prince (c.5th century BCE)

Fertility and birth

WORSHIP OF THE GREAT MOTHER GODDESS, often identified as Earth, has been part of many cultures since the dawn of humanity. For instance, Pacha Mama, the name of the Inca fertility goddess, means "Earth mother". When the Hittite god of farming, Telepinu, withdrew from the world in a rage, and humans began to starve, it was the mother goddess Hannahanna who found him. The myth of the Greek corn goddess Demeter (p.7) and her despairing search for her lost daughter Persephone, during which Earth became a wasteland, was at the heart of Greek religion. Birth and fertility were not exclusively the reserve of goddesses. Frey (p.34) was the Norse god of fertility, a role given in Egypt to the gods Min and Osiris (pp.44, 51, 52); Egyptian mothers sought the help of the impish god Bes at childbirth.

EQUESTRIAN EPONA
Epona, the Celtic horse goddess, is closely linked to the triple mother goddesses, who are often shown nursing babies. Like them, Epona is portrayed with corn and other fertility symbols, but she was especially associated with horse breeding. Horse breeding was crucial because the Celts farmed with horses, and without them they could not have grown enough food.

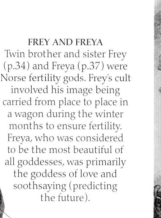

FREY AND FREYA
Twin brother and sister Frey (p.34) and Freya (p.37) were Norse fertility gods. Frey's cult involved his image being carried from place to place in a wagon during the winter months to ensure fertility. Freya, who was considered to be the most beautiful of all goddesses, was primarily the goddess of love and soothsaying (predicting the future).

Frey holds his beard, a symbol of growth, in one hand

Goddess Freya in her chariot

JADE SKIRT
Chalchiuhtlicue, She of the Jade Skirt, was the central Mexican goddess of lakes and streams and, by association, the goddess of birth. She is sometimes depicted with a pair of babies, one male and one female. Chalchiuhtlicue once flooded Earth, but turned humans into fish so that they were saved.

The water goddess Chalchiutlicue stands in water near a giant centipede

Native American Iroquois corn husk mask, worn in midwinter ceremonies to ensure a good harvest

Alabaster figurine of Ishtar c.300–200 BCE

Baby Horus

LOVE GODDESS
Ishtar (p.33), the Babylonian goddess of love, descended to the underworld to rescue her dead husband Tammuz, god of plants. But she was killed, and without Tammuz the whole world withered. Ishtar was brought back to life, but for six months of each year Tammuz must live in the underworld while Ishtar laments. When he rises in the spring, all rejoice.

ISIS AND HORUS
The Egyptian goddess Isis (p.26) is often shown as the perfect mother, nursing the infant Horus (pp.13, 26). When he was only a baby, Horus was bitten by scorpions and would have died, but Isis's cries of anguish halted the Sun god Ra (pp.13, 44, 56, 57) in his journey across the sky. Ra then sent the god Thoth to cure the child.

FIRST MOTHER
Native Americans of the northeast tell how First Father was born from the foam on the sea, and First Mother from the dew on the leaf. The human race increased, but eventually came a time of famine. Then First Mother, who had said, "My strength shall be felt all over Earth", asked to be killed and buried. From her flesh grew the first corn.

Mould for making the casting of Venus (right)

WILLENDORF GODDESS
This stone figurine from Willendorf, Austria, represents a mother goddess and dates from the Neolithic period (c.5000 BCE). The exaggerated curves in this statue of the great mother goddess stress women's role in human fertility.

VENUS AND APHRODITE
Venus (p.40), the Roman goddess of love, beauty, and fertility, seems to have originally been a goddess of farmland and gardens before being identified with Aphrodite, the Greek goddess. Aphrodite was concerned only with love; marriage was the reponsibility of Hera, and childbirth of Hera's daughter Ilithyia.

Children of the gods

Matsya, the fish

Kurma, the turtle

IN MANY MYTHOLOGIES, the gods reproduce just as human beings do. Their children may be other gods (who may even take over from them) or semi-divine heroes, such as Cuchulain and Heracles. Some supreme deities, such as the Norse god Odin (p.37) and the Greek god Zeus (p.16), are called "all-father" in recognition of the role they play in relation to other beings. However, not all children of the gods are good for the world. For instance, the Norse god Loki (p.30) gave birth to the fierce wolf Fenrir and Hel, the mistress of the underworld; while the Greek god of the sea, Poseidon (pp.19, 21), fathered the brutal cyclops Polyphemus. Gods can also incarnate themselves in human or animal form, as the Hindu god Vishnu (pp.11, 18) does in his various guises, such as Narasimha, the half man, half lion; and Vamana, the dwarf.

INCARNATIONS OF VISHNU
The Hindu god Vishnu, the Preserver, has been incarnated nine times in different forms, known as avatars. As the fish, Vishnu saved Manu (p.18), the first man, from the great flood. As the turtle, he helped the gods churn the ocean and win the elixir of immortality. Vishnu raised Earth out of the sea as Varaha, the boar. And as the hero Rama, he rescued his wife from a demon. Vishnu's 10th avatar, Kalki, the horse, will come to destroy and recreate the world at the end of this cycle of time.

Varaha, the boar

Cuchulain rides his chariot into battle

FATHER OF THE PHARAOHS
Falcon-headed Horus (pp.13, 25), whose eyes were the Sun and the Moon, was the child of the Egyptian gods Isis and Osiris. He was conceived when Isis breathed life into the mummified Osiris, who had been murdered by his brother Seth. The long battle between Horus and Seth was vicious, but eventually Horus prevailed. The Egyptian pharaohs, who traced their descent from him, were called the Living Horus.

UGLY WARRIOR
Cuchulain, a hero of Irish mythology, was a fierce warrior. His father was the Sun god Lugh. Although normally very handsome, on the battlefield Cuchulain became a monster. One eye disappeared into his head, while the other bulged; his heels turned to the front; and his jaws opened wide enough to swallow an enemy's head. Before he was killed, Cuchulain strapped himself to a standing stone so that he would die standing up.

Prince Rama

THE WATER TWINS
The Dogon people of Mali in west Africa say that the creator spirit Amma first mated with Earth, and the Nommo (water) twins were born. Human on the top half and snake-like on the bottom half, the twins were made out of the life force of Amma. The Nommo were green in colour, and clothed their mother Earth with plants and trees. They are believed to make an outline of every newborn soul, giving it a twin nature, both male and female.

The Nommo stand between Earth and the sky with their arms outstretched on this Dogon leader's stool

HEROIC HERACLES
The Greek hero Heracles (Hercules in Latin) was the son of Zeus by a mortal woman, Alcmene. As an infant he proved his divine nature by strangling two deadly serpents sent by Zeus's jealous wife Hera. Hera's hatred pursued Heracles all his life, robbing him of his destined throne.

Scary monsters

Giants are found throughout mythology. Their size makes them terrifying, but often they are portrayed as slow, stupid, and easily outwitted. For example, the cyclops Polyphemus believed that the hero Odysseus's name was Nobody. When Odysseus blinded him by stabbing a red-hot poker into his single eye, he yelled out: "Nobody is hurting me!" Polyphemus's father, Poseidon, persecuted Odysseus, wrecking his ships and keeping him from his home for 10 long years.

Cyclopes had only one eye

Fierce incisors tear meat from the bone

ONE-EYED OGRE
Polyphemus was one of the one-eyed giants known as cyclopes. The skulls of mastodons (extinct elephant-like mammals) were once thought to be those of cyclopes.

Mastodon skull

Cyclopes had ferocious appetites and could devour whole carcasses at one sitting

Tunic made from the hides of the Cyclops's prey

Cyclopes tore their prey limb from limb

Ancestor worship

I**N MANY CULTURES, FEAR OF THE EVIL POWER** of spirits of the dead is balanced by a belief in the protective power of the spirits of ancestors, who are thought to watch over and guide the living. For this reason, offerings may be made to ancestor shrines.

For example, in China the head of a family must make regular sacrifices of food at the graves of his ancestors; if not, their hungry ghosts may cause trouble. In both China and Japan, wooden tablets inscribed with the names of ancestors are kept in a household shrine. The duty that the living owe to the dead was never more pressing than in ancient Egypt, where it was vital that the eldest living son of deceased parents raised a monument to their memory. He had to pronounce their names every time he passed it, to keep their names alive.

ROMULUS AND REMUS
Romulus was the mythical founder of Rome; his name simply means "Roman". The twins Romulus and Remus were the sons of the war god Mars. Abandoned as babies, they were suckled by a wolf and raised by a shepherd. The brothers argued about who should found Rome, and Romulus killed Remus with a spade. But Romulus was soon swept off to heaven by his father, where he became a god and was worshipped by the citizens of Rome.

Bronze Yoruba figurine from Benin, west Africa

Female figure, Middle Sepik River, Papua New Guinea

Procession of Oshun devotees

OSHUN WORSHIP
Ancestors are worshipped in many parts of Africa, and are prayed to for good health, fertility, and good fortune. The Yoruba people of west Africa worship Oshun, goddess of the river that bears the same name. Oshun was married to the thunder god Shango, and has human descendants. People bathe in the Oshun River to protect themselves from disease. Women, in particular, consult the goddess Oshun in cases of family problems or illness.

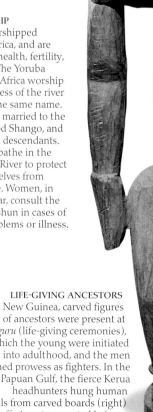

LIFE-GIVING ANCESTORS
In New Guinea, carved figures of ancestors were present at *moguru* (life-giving ceremonies), at which the young were initiated into adulthood, and the men gained prowess as fighters. In the Papuan Gulf, the fierce Kerua headhunters hung human skulls from carved boards (right) as offerings to ancestral beings.

COLOSSAL CHIEFS

On Rapa Nui (Easter Island), a remote and barren island of volcanic rock stranded in the eastern Pacific Ocean, stand hundreds of monolithic stone figures. They are *moai* – figures of dead chiefs who were regarded as descendants of the gods.

FEAST OF LANTERNS

The Bon festival, held in Japan each July, is known as the Feast of Lanterns. It is held in honour of the spirits of the dead, which return to Earth for the three days of the festival. Relatives of the deceased pray at shrines, where they leave food and other treats for the spirits to feast on.

DREAMING ANCESTORS

The Dreamtime is the eternal present in which the revered ancestors of the Australian Aborigines exist, constantly creating the world. Creation story designs, shown to the Aborigines by the ancestors, are still painted on bodies, rocks, and bark, as in this painting from Arnhem Land, North Australia. Aborigines also carve pictures showing events in the Dreamtime on sacred wooden and stone artefacts called *churinga*. These objects embody ancestral spiritual power, and must not be seen by women or the uninitiated.

Papuan ancestral tablet, or ceremonial board

Aboriginal stone knife, similar to those used by the eternal ancestors to create humans

Bark sheath

Evil forces

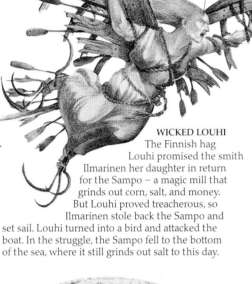

Gap-toothed Louhi as an eagle-woman

WICKED LOUHI
The Finnish hag Louhi promised the smith Ilmarinen her daughter in return for the Sampo – a magic mill that grinds out corn, salt, and money. But Louhi proved treacherous, so Ilmarinen stole back the Sampo and set sail. Louhi turned into a bird and attacked the boat. In the struggle, the Sampo fell to the bottom of the sea, where it still grinds out salt to this day.

BESIDES GODS OF DEATH and sterility, there are many demons and forces of evil in world mythology. Balanced against these are forces of good that came into being to rid the world of evil. In Siberia it is told how the creator Ulgan made himself a companion, Erlik, from mud floating on the primal ocean. But Erlik, jealous of Ulgan, saved mud to try to build his own world, and breathed life into humankind without Ulgan's permission. For these betrayals, Erlik was banished to the underworld, where he sits surrounded by evil spirits. Evil beings are also very active in Hindu mythology, which has many anti-gods and demons. One of the most fearsome of all evil spirits is the Mayan Vucub-Caquix, a monster macaw who claimed to be both the Sun and the Moon. He was killed in a terrible battle by the hero twins Hunahpu and Xbalanque, though not before he had torn off Hunahpu's arm.

TREACHEROUS TRICKSTER
Loki, the Norse trickster god, turned against the other gods and brought about the death of Balder the Beautiful, son of the god Odin (p.37). For this, he is bound in agony, with poison dripping onto his face, until the final battle of Ragnarok, when he will lead an army from Hel (the underworld) against the gods in a ship made from dead men's nails.

Vajrapani holds a thunderbolt in his right hand

Tibetan statue of Vajrapani in his ferocious form

Fiery headdress encrusted with turquoise

DESTROYER OF EVIL
The Tibetan Vajrapani destroys the wicked with his *vajra* (thunderbolt), which spits lightning. One of eight main bodhisattvas, or Buddhist saints, Vajrapani shares characteristics with Indra, the Hindu god of the skies.

Vajrapani, the wielder of the thunderbolt, is a symbol of law and order

Baba Yaga uses her massive pestle (grinding stick) to stir up storms and spread disease

CANNIBAL WITCH
Baba Yaga is the cannibal witch of Russian myth. She lives in a revolving hut supported by hen's feet, and flies through the air in a huge mortar (grinding pot). Her male equivalent is Koshchei the Deathless, who abducts maidens, and can turn into a dragon.

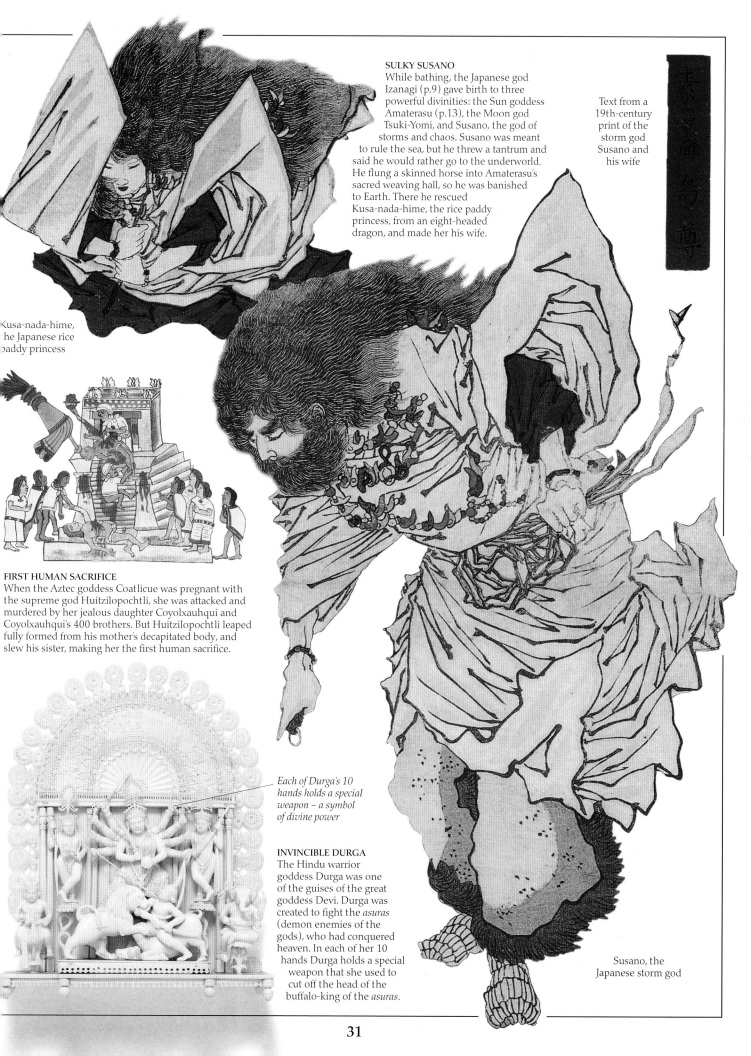

SULKY SUSANO

While bathing, the Japanese god Izanagi (p.9) gave birth to three powerful divinities: the Sun goddess Amaterasu (p.13), the Moon god Tsuki-Yomi, and Susano, the god of storms and chaos. Susano was meant to rule the sea, but he threw a tantrum and said he would rather go to the underworld. He flung a skinned horse into Amaterasu's sacred weaving hall, so he was banished to Earth. There he rescued Kusa-nada-hime, the rice paddy princess, from an eight-headed dragon, and made her his wife.

Text from a 19th-century print of the storm god Susano and his wife

Kusa-nada-hime, the Japanese rice paddy princess

FIRST HUMAN SACRIFICE

When the Aztec goddess Coatlicue was pregnant with the supreme god Huitzilopochtli, she was attacked and murdered by her jealous daughter Coyolxauhqui and Coyolxauhqui's 400 brothers. But Huitzilopochtli leaped fully formed from his mother's decapitated body, and slew his sister, making her the first human sacrifice.

Each of Durga's 10 hands holds a special weapon – a symbol of divine power

INVINCIBLE DURGA

The Hindu warrior goddess Durga was one of the guises of the great goddess Devi. Durga was created to fight the *asuras* (demon enemies of the gods), who had conquered heaven. In each of her 10 hands Durga holds a special weapon that she used to cut off the head of the buffalo-king of the *asuras*.

Susano, the Japanese storm god

Superheroes

MEN AND WOMEN WHO ACHIEVE great feats of daring and courage are celebrated in all mythologies. Often, they are said to be the children of gods, or to be specially favoured by the gods. Some heroes can defeat a whole series of enemies in single combat, and rid countries of the monsters that plague them. Others, such as the Native American hero Hiawatha, are celebrated as peacemakers rather than as warriors. A typical hero is the Tibetan Gesar, who was a god chosen to be born as a man to rid the world of demons. Gesar became a powerful warrior king, with an immortal horse that flew through the sky and spoke all languages. At the end of his life, Gesar retired to heaven, but one day he will return, for evil can never be wholly defeated.

Polynices's corpse is left to rot

BRAVE ANTIGONE
Antigone was the daughter of Oedipus, King of Thebes, Greece. After his death, his two sons, Eteocles and Polynices, fought over the throne and killed each other. Creon, their uncle, buried Eteocles with honour, but threw the body of Polynices out to rot, regarding him as a traitor. Although threatened with death, Antigone bravely defied her uncle and gave Polynices a token burial, sprinkling three handfuls of dust over the corpse. Creon then walled her up in a cave without food or water, so she hanged herself.

When Krishna plays his magic flute, women within earshot join him to dance

Krishna is always blue, which shows that he is an incarnation of Vishnu

Krishna stands on a lotus flower, symbol of Earth

Native Americans made wampum (bead) belts to mark peace agreements

Beads are made from white and purple clam shells

PEACEMAKER
Dekanah-wida was born to bring tidings of peace from the Chief of the Sky Spirits to five warring Native American tribes. Dekanah-wida made the Mohawk chief, Hiawatha, his peacemaker. Hiawatha then travelled between the tribes, persuading them to form the Iroquois League, whose members swore to live in peace together.

DEMON DODGER
Krishna is the eighth avatar (incarnation) of the Hindu god Vishnu (pp.11, 18, 26), and is worshipped as a god in his own right. When he was a child, his mother took him to the countryside to escape the demon king Kansa, who was persecuting them. Kansa sent a female demon to poison him, but Krishna sucked the life out of her instead.

Sigurd kills the dragon

DRAGON SLAYER
The Scandinavian hero Sigurd slew the dragon Fafnir so that he could claim its treasure. Sigurd had been urged to kill the dragon by Regin, Fafnir's brother, who asked Sigurd to return with the dragon's heart. But Regin was plotting to kill Sigurd and steal the treasure for himself. Some birds tried to warn Sigurd, but he could not understand them. Fortunately, as he cooked the dragon's heart he burned his thumb and, putting it into his mouth, tasted the dragon's blood. The blood enabled Sigurd to understand the birds. Learning that Regin meant to betray him, Sigurd killed him and kept the treasure.

Fafnir the dragon

When Yi shot the Suns, they fell to Earth in the shape of crows

The Minotaur had a bull's head on a man's body

MONSTER KILLER

Theseus was the greatest Athenian hero, said to be the son of the Greek sea god Poseidon (pp.19, 21, 26). His most famous feat was slaying the Minotaur, which was part man, part bull. King Minos of Crete regularly fed the Minotaur with Athenian children. Theseus volunteered to be fed to the Minotaur. With the help of Minos's daughter Ariadne, he killed the Minotaur in the labyrinth (maze) in which it lived.

Yi won a potion of immortality, but Chang E drank it herself and floated to the Moon

YI THE ARCHER

The Chinese say that originally there were 10 Suns – sons of the Emperor of the Eastern Heavens. The Suns took it in turns to light the sky. But once all 10 went out to play. Together they were so hot that Earth was scorched, so the Emperor sent Yi, the heavenly archer, to teach them a lesson. Yi shot down nine of them. The Emperor was so upset that he stripped Yi and his wife, Chang E, of their immortality and banished them from heaven.

Heavenly gates are guarded by two soldiers

Mortals on their way to heaven to become immortals

Perseus holds Medusa's severed head

GREEK GUARDIAN

Perseus was the son of the Greek god Zeus and the maiden Danaë. To save his mother from an unwanted marriage, Perseus agreed to fetch the head of the Gorgon Medusa (pp.36, 47), whose glance turned the onlooker to stone. Using a bronze shield as a mirror so that he did not have to meet the Gorgon's gaze, Perseus cut off her head. He then used the head to turn his mother's unwelcome suitor to stone.

Kneeling men and women mourn for the dead

Altars full of food

Gilgamesh clutches a captured lion cub

KING GILGAMESH

Gilgamesh was the great hero of ancient Mesopotamia. He was a semi-divine king who fought monsters with his friend Enkidu (p.44). When Gilgamesh scorned the love of the goddess Ishtar (p.25) she sent a great bull to destroy him, but Gilgamesh and Enkidu slew the bull.

Scenes of the underworld

Chinese funeral banner, 2nd century BCE

Medusa lies dead at Perseus's feet

Divine weapons

Sword, spear, axe, or bow, the weapons of the gods often mirror those of humans. For example, the Norse all-father Odin (p.37) had a magical spear that he used to stir up war. But the gods can also unleash natural forces as weapons, most notably the thunderbolt (lightning), which has been a weapon of sky gods all over the world. Weapons could be improvised out of anything: the club of the semi-divine Greek hero Heracles (p.26) was simply an uprooted olive tree. The Hero Twins of Native American Navajo stories were given bows with arrows of lightning by their father, the Sun god, to help them rid the world of monsters. Even when caught without their weapons, gods can punish the insolent or wicked. When the Greek hunter Actaeon spied the goddess Artemis (p.12) bathing without her bow and arrows, she turned him into a stag and let his own hounds maul him to death.

The Greek god Zeus wields a thunderbolt

BATTLING BROTHERS
This 19th-century chief's axe is a symbol of Tane (pp.11, 23), Oceanic god of the forests, who was himself shaped by craftsmen with axes. After Tane separated Earth and sky, he and his brother Tangaroa (p.15), the god of the seas, began a fierce battle. Tangaroa lashed the land with his waves, trying to wash it away. Tane supplied men with canoes, spears, fish-hooks, and nets to catch Tangaroa's fish. Craftsmen pray to Tane to put their axes to sleep at night, and to wake them up in the morning.

Shango looks both ways so that no one can escape him

THUNDER AND LIGHTNING
The terrifying energy of an electrical storm has been interpreted by many people as the anger of the gods. Thunderbolts have been used as weapons by many gods, including Zeus of ancient Greece (p.16). Native Americans revere the Thunderbird, which produces thunder by flapping its wings, and lightning by flashing its eyes. Tupan, an Amazonian thunder god, caused thunder and lightning by crossing the sky in a dugout canoe.

SPITTER OF THUNDERBOLTS
Ceremonial staffs such as this symbolize Shango, the thunder god of the Yoruba people of west Africa. His symbol is the double axe, which represents thunderbolts. Shango originally was a king, and was given the power to spit thunderbolts by the trickster god Eshu (pp.38, 42). Being hit by lightning is thought to be a sign of Shango's anger.

To terrify Shango's enemies, his devotees hold thunderbolt staffs as they dance to loud drumbeats

MAGICAL SWORD
The Norse god Frey (p.24) had a sword that would fight on its own. But he gave the sword to Skirnir, his servant, as a reward for winning him the hand of the beautiful maiden Gerd. It is said that at the final battle of Ragnarok, Frey will fight the fire giant Surt, who has a blade that flames like the Sun. But without his sword, Frey will be defeated, allowing Surt to burn up the world.

Iron sword from Denmark

ANCESTRAL WEAPON
The boomerang was an important weapon of the Australian Aborigines. The first boomerang represented the Aboriginal Rainbow Snake, and is said to have been made from the tree between heaven and Earth. A myth of the Binbinga tribe of Australia tells how the ancestral snake Bobbi-Bobbi made the first boomerang from one of his ribs.

Rainbow Snake

Aboriginal war boomerangs are designed to fly in straight lines and travel great distances

17th-century brass *vajras* from Tibet, representing thunderbolts

Tibetans use vajras, believed to hold magical powers, in rituals and while meditating

BLADE OF IRON
Ogun is the god of iron and war among the Yoruba people of west Africa. When Earth was still a watery waste, Ogun used to climb down from heaven on a spider's web to hunt in the marshland. After Earth was formed, Ogun cleared the land with his iron blade. He was last seen sinking into the ground with his sword.

Ritual sword used in Ogun worship

Vows taken in the name of Ogun, with the tongue on a blade or some other iron object, are completely binding

Ceremonial bow and arrows

GODDESS OF HUNTING
Diana (p.12) is the Roman name for Artemis, the Greek goddess of hunting and archery. Although Diana was the goddess of the hunt, she was also the protector of all wild animals.

Diana, Roman protector of wild animals

Silver replica of Thor's hammer from Denmark

THOR'S LUCKY HAMMER
The Norse thunder god Thor was the son of the all-father Odin; his mother was Earth. He had a wonderful hammer, Mjollnir, which never missed its target when thrown, and always returned to his hand. Vikings wore pendants in the shape of Thor's hammer for protection. Large replicas of these lucky hammers were also used to bless weddings, births, and funerals.

Thor in his chariot pulled by goats

Gods of war

HUMAN HISTORY HAS BEEN SHAPED by war and conflict, and gods of war have a high status in many mythologies. The ancient Greeks had two war gods: Ares, who was the god of fighting, and Athena, who was the goddess of strategy. That a goddess should take an interest in warfare is not unusual. Ishtar (p.25) was the Mesopotamian goddess of both love and war; the Irish war goddess, the Morrigan could change into a crow, and settled in that form on the shoulder of the dying hero Cuchulain (p.26). But most war gods are male, and many of them, like Ares and Odin, are bloodthirsty, revelling in slaughter.

GREEK GODDESS OF STRATEGY
While Ares was the Greek god of fighting, Athena was the goddess of strategy and wisdom. She sprang from the head of her father Zeus (p.16), fully armed and ready for battle. Athena is always depicted in full armour, with the head of the gorgon Medusa (pp.33, 47) fixed to her breastplate.

The divine blacksmith Gu taught the first humans how to make tools so that they could work the land

Mars wears a warrior's helmet

PROTECTIVE MARS
Mars was the Roman god of war. He seems to have originally been a god of agriculture, and even as a war god he retained a protective function, unlike his brutal and violent Greek equivalent, Ares. He was one of the most important Roman gods, and was believed to have fathered Romulus, the founder of Rome. Soldiers made sacrifices to Mars before and after battle.

GOD OF IRON
Gu was the fifth-born child of Mawu-Lisa (pp.14, 16), the west African creator god. Mawu-Lisa gave her strength to Gu. He is made of iron, and is sometimes depicted as an iron sword. In this form, Mawu-Lisa used him to clear Earth for humans to live on. Gu is the god of iron, and consequently of war, since war is waged with iron weapons.

Iron statue of Gu, war god of the Fon people of west Africa

WARRING KU
Ku was the war god of Hawaii. He had many names descriptive of his various roles. As patron of woodworkers he was Ku-Adzing-Out-The-Canoe. When the gods were trapped between their parents Earth and sky, Ku-Of-The-Angry-Face wanted to kill them, but the other gods fought Ku. This was the beginning of warfare.

FIGHTING SPIRITS
The valkyries of the Viking (Norse) god Odin were female spirits who rode to battle to give victory or death, according to Odin's will. They also waited on the souls of dead warriors in the hall of Valhalla (heaven). The name valkyrie means "chooser of the slain". The Viking fertility goddess Freya (p.24) was said to ride to battle and claim half the slain.

Valkyries rode horses to fetch dead warriors from the battlefield and take them to Odin's Valhalla

Norse all-father Odin sacrificed one of his eyes in return for wisdom

Chinese bronze sword, 4th century BCE

NORSE WAR GODS
The Viking (Norse) gods were among the most warlike of all. Their leader, Odin (left), was the god of battle, inspiring his *berserker* warriors with a fighting frenzy. Only those who died in battle joined him in Valhalla (the Viking heaven) after death.

Spears were among a Viking warrior's most prized possessions

DEMON KILLER
Skanda, the six-headed Hindu god of war, is the son of Shiva. He was born to kill the demon Taraka, who had been oppressing the gods. Skanda rides a peacock, on which he travelled around the world in a contest of learning with Ganesha (p.38), his brother. Ganesha, who stayed at home and read, knew more than Skanda when he returned.

CHINESE WARRIOR GOD
Guan Di is the Chinese god of war. Originally a humble seller of tofu (soybean curd), he devoted himself to study, and is still regarded as a patron of literature. However, after he killed a magistrate, he had to flee his home and fend for himself. Guan Di became a soldier, one of the three famous Brothers of the Peach Orchard. In 1594 CE, he was elevated to the status of god of war.

Statue of Guan Di, the Chinese god of war

Contacting the spirits

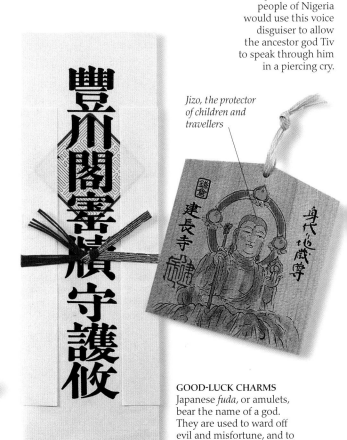

THE ANCIENT GREEKS TOOK THEIR PROBLEMS to the oracle of Apollo at Delphi, where a priestess called the Pythia (Pythoness) went into a trance and uttered strange words that were then interpreted by a priest. Among the Vikings, *volvas* (prophetesses) answered questions in a similar way. Siberian shamans, Native American medicine men, and Australian Aboriginal karadji, or clever men, all use drumming, dance, and song to enter an altered mental state in which they can communicate with the spirit world. Offerings and sacrifices may also bridge the gap between the two worlds, as when worshippers are possessed by the gods in voodoo rites. Among the Yoruba of west Africa, the god of fate, Eshu (p.42), uses sacrifices to plead with the other gods, or to appease evil spirits on behalf of humanity.

GUIDING GOD
The Greek god Hermes (Mercury in Rome) was the messenger of the gods, and also the guide of souls into the underworld. As he was always going to and fro, he became the protector of all travellers.

Pipe of carved human bone

Priest speaks into this hole to distort his voice and make it boom out

VOICE DISGUISER
A priest of the Tiv people of Nigeria would use this voice disguiser to allow the ancestor god Tiv to speak through him in a piercing cry.

Half-halo represents Ganesha's divinity

Noose to trap delusion

Jizo, the protector of children and travellers

GOOD-LUCK CHARMS
Japanese *fuda*, or amulets, bear the name of a god. They are used to ward off evil and misfortune, and to bring good luck. They are often placed on household shrines to protect the family.

CONVEYOR OF PRAYERS
Ganesha, the wise elephant-headed son of Shiva (p.50), is the god of all good enterprises. Hindus ask Ganesha to pass on their requests to Shiva. They make offerings to the pot-bellied god before going on a journey, starting a business, or making plans for a wedding.

豊川閣靈檳守護攸

The ancestors sit in the top branches of the world tree; the shaman climbs up to ask for their help

Shaman's spirit helpers often take animal forms

Drumbeats are used to call the spirits that will help the shaman

Metal ornaments hanging from the belt protect against evil spirits

THE SHAMAN
Shamans are believed to have had a life-changing vision that enables them to enter a trance and fly to the spirit world. A shaman's power is usually used for healing, though it may also cause disease or death.

Souls of the unborn nest in the tree

Dancers hung from rawhide thongs sewn through the skin

SUN DANCE
In customs such as the Sun Dance (above), Plains Native Americans performed rituals involving excruciating pain as sacrifices to the Great Spirit. Once they had performed the ritual, the dancers hoped to receive a vision.

The pipe bowl is round, like the world, and outside lies the endless Universe

38457

PIPES OF PEACE
The sacred pipe is an important part of many Native American rituals, bringing peace and healing. Tobacco was believed to have the power to summon good spirits, ward off evil ones, and bring either good or bad luck. Communal smoking helped to reinforce the ties between families, tribes, and the Universe.

Tiger spirits often teach shamans their craft

Spirit

The world tree houses all souls

Siberian shaman's outfit

Love, fortune, and happiness

MANY PEOPLE WORSHIP DEITIES who will bring them luck in life. In ancient times, for example, the Romans had a cult of the goddess Fortuna (Good Luck). The Ewe people of Togo in west Africa believe that the soul of each unborn child must first visit Ngolimeno, the Mother of the Spirit People. If they please her, she will grant them a happy life. The Japanese worship Seven Gods of Luck, of whom one, Benten, is a goddess. But the Chinese worship many gods of fortune and happiness. The lucky Ho-Ho twins (right) are often shown attending Tsai Shen, the god of wealth. Another common trio is Fu Shen, god of happiness; Lu Shen, god of good luck; and Shou Shen, god of long life.

THE WINGED GOD
Cupid (Eros in Greek) was the mischievous Roman god of love, often shown as a cheeky infant with a bow and arrows. Some of his arrows had gold tips and caused people to fall in love; others were tipped with lead and had the opposite effect.

Detail from Botticelli's famous painting *The Birth of Venus* (c.1486)

BORN OF FOAM
The Greek goddess of love and desire, Aphrodite (p.25), known as Venus to the Romans, was born from the foam of the sea. She devoted herself to pleasure, prided herself on never doing any work, and was often assisted by Eros (Cupid to the Romans). Aphrodite was married to the smith god Hephaestus, but had many lovers among both gods and men. As Venus she was the mother of the Roman hero Aeneas.

Each twin carries a jar containing a lotus of purity and perfection

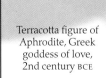

Terracotta figure of Aphrodite, Greek goddess of love, 2nd century BCE

Born from the foam of the sea, Aphrodite floated ashore on a scallop shell

The gods are standing on beds of lotus flowers

The head of each twin is decorated with a lotus

GOOD FORTUNE GODS
The Japanese Seven Gods of Luck (Shichi Fukujin) are Bishamon, Daikoku, Ebisu, Fukurokuju, Hotei, Jorojin, and the goddess Benten – the bringer of happiness, love, and good fortune. The Shichi Fukujin are often shown together on their treasure ship. Their treasures include a hat of invisibility, a lucky rain hat, keys to the divine treasure house, a purse that never empties, a cloak of feathers, rolls of silk, and scrolls or books.

Benten rides an ox, a symbol of good fortune

CONFUSED DEITY
Kwan-non is the god or goddess of mercy in Japanese Buddhism. Priests regard Kwan-non as a male divinity, but most people pray to him as a goddess, and he appears in 33 female forms. This statue shows her (or him) holding a baby. Expectant mothers would pray to this statue as Koyasu Kwan-non (Kwan-non of Easy Childbirth).

The Ho-Ho gods, symbolizing happy relations between couples

Love medicines are inserted into pockets on the chest of each doll

LOVE DOLLS
These Native American medicine dolls are used by the Menominee of the western Great Lakes to ensure that a husband and wife remain faithful to each other. The male doll is named after the husband and the female doll after the wife, and the two are tied together face to face. The Potawatomi, also of the western Great Lakes, used dolls as charms to make one person fall in love with another.

HO-HO TWINS
The two immortals called Ho are the patrons of Chinese merchants. Besides bringing prosperity, they represent harmonious union between couples, because the word *ho* means harmony. Their names were originally Han Shan and Shih-teh. Han Shan was a holy fool who attached himself to the monastery at Kuo-ching Ssu. The monks rejected him, but Shih-teh, an orphan in the kitchens, saved scraps to feed him.

Tricksters

LIGHT-HEARTED COMEDY and dark humour are introduced into myths by trickster figures, such as the Native American Coyote (left), whose insatiable curiosity and love of mischief leave havoc and confusion in their wake. Tricksters may be animal, human, or both. Some tricksters hover between good and evil, such as the wily Norse god Loki (p.30). The Ashanti people of west Africa tell tales of Anansi, the cunning spider-man who won the famous stories of the sky god Nyame (p.17). By a series of clever tricks, Anansi trapped all the creatures that Nyame thought were impossible to catch. For example, he caught the fairy Mmoatia by making a tar baby, to which Mmoatia stuck fast. When Anansi delivered the creatures to Nyame, he was so impressed that he willingly gave Anansi the stories. Since then, the tales have been called spider stories.

WILY COYOTE
Many Native American peoples tell stories of the wily Coyote, who both tricks and is tricked. Coyote has many human characteristics – he is greedy and selfish, and his exploits lead to bad as well as good consequences.

Cowrie shells are used by Eshu to predict the future

MISCHIEVOUS ESHU
Eshu is the trickster god of the Yoruba people of west Africa. His many guises include giant, dwarf, cheeky boy, wise old man, and priest, as seen here. Eshu loves mischief. For example, he broke up a firm friendship between two men by wearing a hat that was white on one side but black on the other, causing them to quarrel about its colour.

Eshu holds a small statue of himself

Mask worn to impersonate Hare

Hare climbs up the mask

CUNNING HARE
Hare is an African animal trickster who became known in America as Brer Rabbit. Cunning and wily, Hare always outwits the other animals, except when Tortoise challenged him to a race. Instead of running, Tortoise placed members of his family all around the course and sat waiting for Hare at the finish line.

Figures represent Eshu in his various guises

An Eshu priest would wear this statue by hooking the headdress over his shoulder, just as Eshu is doing with the statue he is holding

Medicine calabashes (bowls) represent Eshu's magical powers

SUN CATCHER
Maui-Of-A-Thousand-Tricks is the trickster hero of Polynesian mythology. He fished up the islands with his magical hook; pushed up the heavens; stole fire for humankind; and snared the Sun with his sister's hair to slow it down, ensuring that we have long summer days.

The tengu rescue the hero Tametomo from the jaws of a giant fish

INVISIBLE TRICKSTERS
The tengu are Japanese trickster spirits, part bird, part man. They are said to be descended from the storm god Susano (p.31), who himself got into trouble by playing tricks. The tengu have magic cloaks of invisibility.

The fish represents the islands that Maui fished up from the sea

GRIMACING GOD
Bes was a popular god of music, dance, and laughter in ancient Egypt. His grimacing face and comical antics were thought to frighten away evil spirits. He was the protector of mothers in childbirth and the companion of young children. He is always shown sticking his tongue out at the world.

Bacchus's long, flowing hair shows his eternal youth

INDULGENT GOD
Bacchus (Dionysus in Greek) was the Roman god of wine and ecstasy. His followers were wild women called the Maenads (Frenzied Ones). When sailors captured Bacchus, his tricks sent them diving madly into the sea, where they turned into dolphins. It was Bacchus who gave King Midas the double-edged gift of turning all that he touched into gold.

Animal idols

Gods and spirits may be shown in animal form or as half human, half beast. Trickster figures, such as the African spider-man Anansi, may be a man, an animal, or a mixture of both at different times in the same story. Some gods have an animal helper, such as the fox that lived with the Japanese rice god Inari (p.22) and acted as his messenger. Other gods can transform themselves into animals. The Greek god Zeus (p.16), for example, became a bull and then a swan while pursuing his love affairs. Gods sometimes have an animal double – the Aztec god Quetzalcoatl (p.16) had a twin called Xolotl, a dog who helped bring the bones of humankind back from the underworld.

Celtic drinking horns tipped with sheeps' heads

THE HORNED ONE
Gods with animals' horns are found in many mythologies. One of the most famous was the Celtic horned god Cernunnos, who was lord of the beasts and a god of fertility. The goat's horns of the Greek god Pan (p.22) probably inspired pictures of the Christian Devil.

Nagas, sacred snakes, have both protective and destructive powers

THE BULL OF HEAVEN
This winged bull stood guard over a royal palace in Assyria. The bull was a cult animal all over ancient west Asia. For example, a bull of heaven was sent to destroy the Sumerian hero Gilgamesh (pp.13, 33). But Gilgamesh and his friend Enkidu slew the bull, and gave its heart to the Sun god Shamash.

Half human, half beast

In many cultures the gods are depicted as half human, half animal. This is especially true of the ancient Egyptian gods, nearly all of whom have at least one animal form. For example, the cow goddess Hathor was also worshipped as the lioness Sekhmet and the cat Bastet, while the dog or jackal god Anubis could also become a snake or a falcon. The Sun god Ra (pp.13, 54, 57) turned himself into a cat to cut off the head of the evil snake Apep, who attacked him every night.

19th-century Sri Lankan mask

Fierce face wards off the evil spirits thought to cause sickness

THE SNAKE DEMON
This mask of Naga Rassa, or Snake Demon, is worn in dances to drive away evil spirits. The nagas (sacred snakes) were descended from the ancient sage Kasyapa, the father of life. Buddhists tell how Mucilinda, a king of the nagas, grew more heads to shelter the Buddha from a storm.

SEKHMET
The Sun god Ra sent the raging lioness Sekhmet to destroy humankind. But when Ra changed his mind, the only way to stop Sekhmet from killing was to make her drunk.

SOBEK
The Egyptian crocodile god Sobek (p.51), son of the creator goddess Neith, was the ever-hungry lord of the waters in the River Nile. He was depicted as a crocodile or as a man with a crocodile's head. As Sobek-Ra, he was an aspect of the Sun god.

ANUBIS
The jackal-headed god Anubis made the first mummy when he wrapped the body parts of the god Osiris (pp.24, 51, 52) in cloth to put them back together. In the underworld, Anubis weighed the hearts of the dead against the feather of justice.

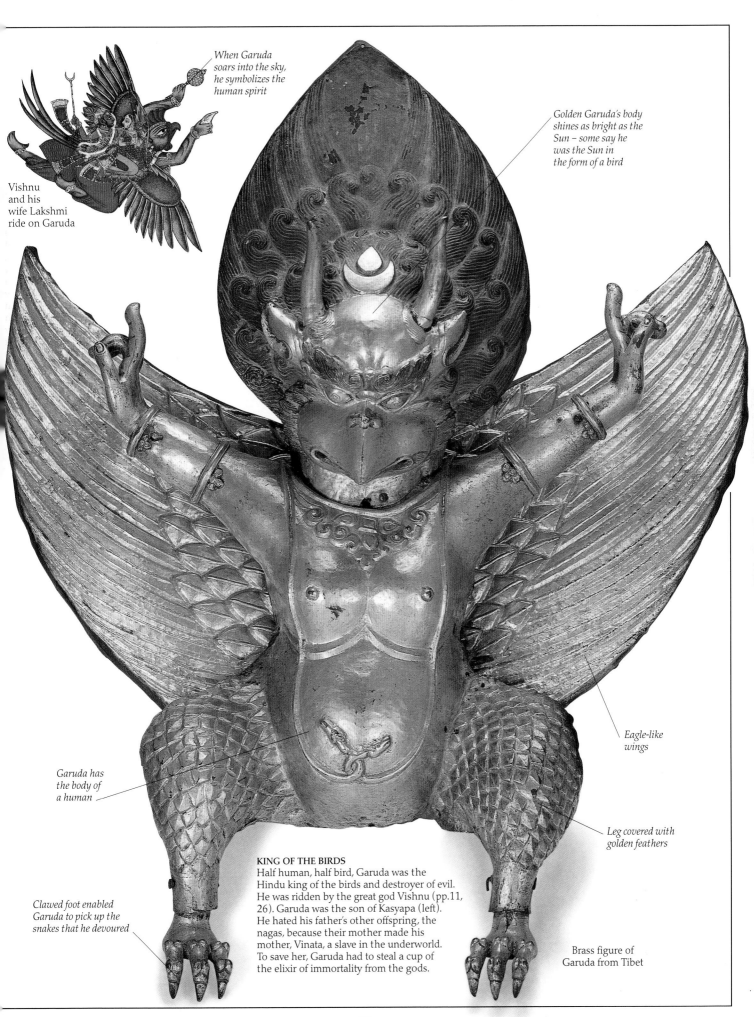

When Garuda soars into the sky, he symbolizes the human spirit

Vishnu and his wife Lakshmi ride on Garuda

Golden Garuda's body shines as bright as the Sun – some say he was the Sun in the form of a bird

Eagle-like wings

Garuda has the body of a human

Leg covered with golden feathers

Clawed foot enabled Garuda to pick up the snakes that he devoured

KING OF THE BIRDS
Half human, half bird, Garuda was the Hindu king of the birds and destroyer of evil. He was ridden by the great god Vishnu (pp.11, 26). Garuda was the son of Kasyapa (left). He hated his father's other offspring, the nagas, because their mother made his mother, Vinata, a slave in the underworld. To save her, Garuda had to steal a cup of the elixir of immortality from the gods.

Brass figure of Garuda from Tibet

Mythical beasts

Stories about mythical creatures are found all over the world. Native Americans say that many monsters peopled the world at the beginning of time, until great heroes defeated them. Some people believe that mythical beasts are based on garbled accounts of real creatures – that unicorns, for example, are really rhinoceroses. But mythical creatures seem to be more a focus for fear, awe, and wonder than simply mistaken identity. Monsters are sometimes combinations of various animals, such as the griffin, which was half eagle, half lion. Just giving an ordinary animal a special feature, such as the ability of the Greek horse Pegasus to fly, transports it from the ordinary world to a realm of wonder.

WILD HORSES
Half man, half horse, the centaur was a wild and savage creature. One exception was Chiron, a wise centaur who was the tutor to many Greek heroes. He died after being accidentally wounded by Heracles (p.26) with a poisoned arrow.

CREATURES OF THE DEEP
In the past, sailors returned from their travels with strange beasts, which they claimed to have fished from the sea. The creature Jenny Haniver (above) is actually a dried skate fish. Some of these curious creatures were created by joining the bodies of different animals together. For example, a monkey's body was grafted onto the tail of a fish to create a merman.

Spiky claws protrude from the dragon's wings

BLOWING HOT AIR
Fire-breathing winged dragons who jealously guard their hoards of treasure feature in many European myths. For example, the Norse (Viking) dragon Fafnir (p.32) was actually a man who turned into a dragon to protect his treasure. Many stories tell of dragon-slaying heroes who rescue maidens, or win their hands in marriage. One example was Tristan, the Celtic hero who killed a dragon to win the hand of Isolde. Unlike the fearsome European dragon, Chinese dragons are kindly and serpent-like.

Dragons breathe fire through their mouths

HORN OF PURITY
The unicorn was a white horse-like creature with a single spiral horn growing from its forehead. It was said that if a unicorn dipped its horn into water, the water would become pure. In fact, the unicorn was such a powerful symbol of purity that supposed unicorn horns (actually the tusks of narwhal whales) once sold for 20 times their weight in gold.

Unicorn horns were prized for their supposed ability to detect poison

DREADFUL LOCKS
The gorgons were three snake-haired sisters, Stheno, Euryale, and Medusa. Stheno and Euryale were immortal, but Medusa was mortal, and was slain by the Greek hero Perseus. Blood that dripped from her severed head over Libya infested the country with snakes.

Ship's emblem depicting the gorgon Medusa

WINGS OF A HERO
The winged horse Pegasus was ridden by the Greek hero Bellerophon. When his enemies ordered Bellerophon to kill the monstrous Chimera (below), they hoped he would die in the attempt. Instead, however, riding Pegasus, Bellerophon swooped down on the monster from above and riddled it with arrows.

Greek coin showing the winged Pegasus

A serpent formed the Chimera's tail

The middle part of the Chimera was a she-goat

European dragons have bat-like wings

HEADS AND TAILS
The Chimera was a fire-breathing monster made up of the body parts of various animals. It was one of the children of the half-nymph, half-serpent Echidna, who also spawned such monsters as the Sphinx and the 100-headed serpent Ladon. The Chimera was slain by the Greek hero Bellerophon.

Thorny hooks protrude from the dragon's tail

The Chimera had the forequarters of a lioness

The dragon's skin is covered with scales like those of a serpent or fish

Clawed feet are seen on both Chinese and European dragons

Painting the story

THERE ARE MANY WAYS of telling stories other than through speech, and many myths are told through ritual, dance, or art rather than through narrative storytelling. In the chantways (right) of the Native American Navajo, sand-painting, song, prayer, dance, and ritual combine to recreate complex myths, which are remembered not for their story content, but for their healing spiritual power. The Australian Aboriginal stories of the Dreamtime are recalled, not just in words and ceremonies, but also through traditional designs painted on the body. The same designs are used in bark paintings, and the ground paintings of central Australia, which are very similar to Navajo sand-paintings.

BEATING THE DRUM
Across Africa, drums are used to beat out rhythms to accompany re-enactment rituals and dances. Drums are thought to have spirits living in them, which may possess those who dance to their beat. The *bata* drum, used by the Yoruba tribe of west Africa in ceremonies to honour the thunder god Shango, is said to have been made by Shango to frighten his enemies.

The headdress varies in size and design, according to the character

Noble characters paint their faces green

Heroes wear red jackets

Wooden snake stick (symbol of lightning)

STORIES THROUGH DANCE
Kathakali dancers enact stories from the two great epics of India, the *Mahabharata* and the *Ramayana*. The essence of both stories is the eternal struggle between good and evil, and dances usually end with the conquering of a demon by a hero.

SNAKE DANCE
Native Americans hold rituals to ensure rain and good crops. In the Hopi Snake Dance, dancers hold live snakes in their mouths. Snake sticks are set up in ceremonial chambers. After the dance, the snakes are released to take the dancers' prayers to the gods.

Beats of the double-sided drum call up new creations

The skirt is made up of many layers of white cotton

Ankle bracelets

RING OF FLAMES
Hindu god Shiva dances the Tandava, which represents the creation and destruction of the world. He dances in a circle of flames – one hand cupping the flame of destruction, the other holding the drum of creation. As he dances, Shiva tramples the dwarf of ignorance beneath his feet.

Mudstone

Sandstone

Gypsum

Chalk

Brown pigment

Yellow pigment

Red pigment

Charcoal

Sacred sand-paintings

The sand-paintings of the Native American Navajo are temporary altars created and destroyed as part of healing rituals known as chantways. Their Navajo name means "place where the gods come and go". Each painting must be re-created in exactly the same way each time, or the ritual will not work.

Only men can become qualified sand-painters

Pigments are trickled onto the sand through the thumb and forefinger

The Oculate Being has bulging eyes

POWDER PAINTS
Sand-painting pigments are gathered by the family sponsoring the ceremony, and ground in a mortar and pestle. Pigments include sandstone, mudstone, charcoal from hard oak, cornmeal, powdered flower petals, and plant pollen.

CHANTWAY CEREMONIES
Sand-paintings are made by skilled painters under the direction of the singer, who oversees the ritual. An average sand-painting takes six men about four hours to complete. When the painting is finished, the singer sprinkles it with protective pollen, says a prayer, and then the ritual begins.

POWERFUL PICTURES
Sand-paintings contain exact depictions of the Navajo Holy People – supernatural beings whose powers are evoked in the chantway ceremonies. Such sand-paintings are sacred and powerful. This non-sacred sand-painting, made for commercial sale, shows a typical Holy Person.

Bracelets and armlets hang from the wrists and elbows

Snake-like tongue

WOVEN STORY
This woven textile from the Paracas people of Peru is full of the spirits and demons of Paracas mythology, including bug-eyed Oculate Beings, shown as heads with no bodies, and long tongues snaking out between prominent teeth.

Alpaca wool weaving from southern Peru, 600–200 BCE

Universal creatures

MANY COMMON THEMES run through world mythology. One theme connects human beings with other animals – we are descended from them, or they are our reincarnated ancestors, or they represent gods or spirits whom we must worship or appease. In many creation myths, such as the Australian Aboriginal stories of the Dreamtime, the first inhabitants of the world are neither animal nor human, but a mixture of both. This is true of many animal gods, such as the African spider-man Anansi. The ancient Egyptian gods all have one or more animal forms as well as human forms. Even in the Judaeo-Christian tradition, the Devil can take the form of a snake.

TURTLE WORLD
Many Native American peoples believe that Earth is supported on the back of a turtle – a belief that is also found in Hindu mythology. In one myth, the creator god Brahma (pp.6, 14, 56) took the shape of a turtle to create the world. Vishnu (p.11, 26) became a turtle to help the gods win the elixir of immortality. In North America and Africa, the turtle is also a trickster figure.

Eyes of inlaid turquoise

Native American Anasazi frog, a symbol of water

THE FROG
A west African story of how Frog brought death into the world is echoed by a Native American myth telling how Frog was so angry with his Maker that he spat poison into the Maker's water, killing him and all his creatures. To the Māoris of New Zealand, the frog was a rain god, an association also made by Native Americans. In Egypt, Heket was a frog goddess of childbirth and resurrection.

Recurring crocodiles

Because of their fearsome appearance, crocodiles appear in many myths, and they are often threatening creatures. For example, the Basuto tribe of Africa believes that a crocodile can seize a man's shadow and pull him under water. But on the island of Sulawesi, in Indonesia, crocodiles are addressed as Grandfather because they may be an ancestor. And it is believed that a crocodile will attack a human only when told to do so by the god Poe Mpalaburu.

Detail from a Papuan shield

Man inside the belly of a crocodile

FATHER CROCODILE
In Papua New Guinea, people believe that crocodiles have magical powers. One myth tells how the creator, Ipila, carved the first four humans from wood, and gave them sago to eat. But two of them began to eat meat, and turned into crocodile-men. The clans descended from them claim the crocodile as their father.

Turquoise mosaic squares

Coral pieces add colour to the nose and mouth

Ceremonial snake pendant worn by priests of the Aztec rain god Tlaloc

LIFE-GIVING SERPENT
The snake is probably the most widely revered creature in world mythology. It is often associated with the primal waters from which all life was created. In the Americas, the double-headed serpent is associated with life-giving rain. Many Australian Aborigines credit the creation of the landscape to the Rainbow Snake, the source of magical power. In west Africa, the Rainbow Snake Aido-Hwedo (pp.14, 56) arches over the sky and under the sea.

**Egyptian
crocodile god
Sobek**

*The crocodile has
large snapping jaws
with very sharp teeth*

**Mayan crocodile
incense burner**

HEAVENLY MONSTER
In Mayan art there are numerous depictions of
the celestial, or cosmic, monster – a being with a
crocodile's body and two heads, one at the front
and one at the back. The monster is sometimes
shown arching
over the heavens,
its body in the
form of clouds.

Clawed feet

**Golden crocodile
figure made by the
Ashanti people of
west Africa**

*Dry, scaly skin
prevents water
loss in the hot
African climate*

Nile
crocodile

*Back feet
are webbed*

*Nile crocodiles
are found on
riverbanks
throughout
tropical Africa*

*Powerful
whip-like tail*

AFRICAN ANCESTORS
Many Africans believe crocodiles
are reincarnated people. In west
Africa it is said that a person who
kills a crocodile will become one.
If someone is attacked by a
crocodile, it is believed that the
victim must have harmed the
crocodile during its human life.

RAVENOUS SOBEK
The ancient Egyptians worshipped
crocodiles in the form of the crocodile
god Sobek (p.44), who was often depicted with
the head of a crocodile and the body of a human.
Sobek was so hungry that, when the dismembered
body of Osiris (pp.44, 52) was thrown into the
River Nile, he ate some of it. The other gods
cut out Sobek's tongue for this wicked act.

Death and the underworld

SINCE HUMANITY BEGAN, people have told stories to explain what happens after death. The Mayan hero twins Hunahpu and Xbalanque descended to Xibalba (the Place of Fright) to rescue their father from One Death, lord of the underworld. The twins survived ordeals in the Houses of Lances, Fire, and Jaguars. They then boasted that they had power over death, and to prove it let themselves be killed and ground like flour. When they came back to life, the lords of death were so impressed that they asked to be killed too. But the twins did not revive them, and so the power of death was lessened forever. In his top hat and dark glasses, the Haitian voodoo god Ghede guards the eternal crossroads, where the souls of the dead pass on their way to the underworld.

The skeleton is commonly used as an image of death

CHINESE JUDGE OF THE DEAD
Yen-lo is the terrifying ruler and judge of the dead in China. First, the souls are weighed: the virtuous are light, the sinful heavy. Then the souls must pass a number of tests and challenges. They are assaulted by demons, attacked by dogs, then allowed one last glimpse of home and family before being given a drink that wipes away all memories. Finally, each soul is reincarnated.

DYING FOR DISOBEDIENCE
The elaborate funeral rites of the Dogon people of west Africa involve dancing and chanting in a secret language. These rituals recount a myth that describes how death entered the world because of the disobedience of young men. Many Africans believe that the spirits of the dead have power over the living.

Osiris, Egyptian god of the underworld

Horus, son of Osiris

Skirts are red to represent death

THE AFTERLIFE
The ancient Egyptians believed that their souls would be weighed against the feather of truth, and that they would then be led into the Hall of the Two Truths to face the lord of the dead, Osiris (pp.44, 51). The virtuous hoped for a new life in the Field of Reeds, a perfected version of Egypt.

AZTEC LORD OF THE UNDERWORLD

Mictlantecuhtli, the Aztec god of death, is usually depicted as a white skeleton spotted with blood. On their way to his peaceful underworld (Mictlan), the dead were reduced to skeletons by a wind of knives. Mictlantecuhtli was said to be the father of Quetzalcoatl (p.16), the lord of life.

The grinning Mictlantecuhtli welcomes the dead to his underworld

DAY OF THE DEAD

The Mexican Day of the Dead (1 November) is an occasion for great festivities. On this day, families in Mexico pray to the souls of dead relatives so that they will return to Earth for one night. Altars in homes and cemeteries are decorated with food, flowers, and ghoulish sugar models. A candle is lit for each soul to help it find its way back to the land of the living. Many other cultures celebrate a day of the dead, including China, which has the Feast of the Hungry Ghosts.

Altar skulls are made from sugar and water, and are decorated with icing sugar

Demons torment the souls of the dead

Depiction of the Christian hell

VISIONS OF HELL

Eternal torment in an underworld, such as the Christian hell, is the fate of sinners in many cultures. The Greeks devised ingenious fates for those who offended the gods. Sisyphus, who told tales on Zeus (p.16), was forced to spend eternity rolling a stone uphill, only to see it roll back to the ground just as he was reaching the top. Tantalus (who served the gods his own son at a banquet) was condemned to stand neck-high in water, with ripe fruit dangling over his head, never able to eat or drink.

Viking chieftains were cremated in longboats to transport them to Valhalla

WARRIOR HEAVEN

Viking (Norse) warriors longed to be chosen for death in battle by Odin's warrior maidens, the Valkyries (p.37). This meant that, instead of going to hell, warriors would experience a glorious afterlife of feasting and fighting in the golden halls of Valhalla (heaven). There they prepare to fight for the gods in the final battle (Ragnarok) of this present world.

White pottery figure of the Aztec lord of death

Sacred sites

THE ICE-AGE cave pictures of Europe – and their ancient equivalents in Australia, America, and Africa – show us that humankind has always recognized and respected sacred spaces, where the everyday and the eternal meet. Sacred sites may be temporary or permanent, and the same place may be re-used many times. Many Christian churches, for example, are on the sites of pagan temples. Lakes, rivers, caves, woods, or mountain tops can be just as spiritual as a temple or church. A place may declare itself sacred simply by its beauty – something the Japanese recognize in erecting *torii* (right) in places that are natural shrines. A totem pole, erected to proclaim a family's mythological descent, is also visible proof that the world of humankind and the world of gods and spirits are one and the same.

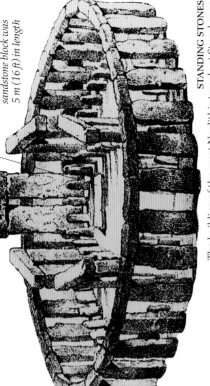

Most probably an altar, this flat sandstone block was 5 m (16 ft) in length

GREAT PYRAMIDS

The Egyptian Sun god Ra (pp.13, 44, 57) was born on a pyramid-shaped piece of land jutting out of the primal ocean. This shape was then adopted by the Egyptian pharaohs (kings) for their tombs, putting them under the protection of the Sun god.

STANDING STONES

The building of the great Neolithic temple at Stonehenge in Wiltshire, UK, occurred between about 2500 and 1500 BCE. The sacred stones, which are aligned with the Sun, Moon, and stars, are thought to have had astronomical connections. Stonehenge was also adopted as a sacred site by the druids, Celtic priests of the Iron Age (c.1100 BCE).

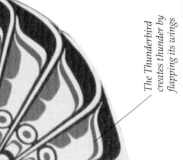

Horizontal bars' curved ends reach up to heaven

ENTRANCE TO HEAVEN

A *torii* is a gateless entranceway that marks the point where ordinary space becomes sacred space. A *torii* stands at the entrance to each Japanese Shinto shrine, and also in front of the sacred Mount Fuji (right). Because *torii* means "bird", it is sometimes said that the *torii* is erected to provide a resting place for birds so that their song will please the gods at dawn.

Thunderbird makes lightning by opening and closing its eyes

The Thunderbird creates thunder by flapping its wings

Mythical monuments

The totem poles of Native Americans are carved heraldic monuments displaying images of a family's or clan's mythological descent. Some wealthy families commissioned totem poles as memorials to their dead relatives. The Native American Kwakiutl people say that the first totem pole, Kakaluyuwish (Pole That Holds Up The Sky), was made by Wakiash, a Kwakiutl chief, with knowledge that he won from the animal-people when Raven flew him around the world.

Thunderbird totem pole in Stanley Park, Vancouver, Canada (1988 copy of an original that was erected in 1927)

TEMPLE OF THE MAIDEN

The ancient Greek word *parthenon* means "temple of the maiden", and the Parthenon was the great temple of Athena (p.36) situated on the Acropolis at Athens, Greece. Athena, the goddess of war and wisdom, was the patron of the city. The Parthenon contained her statue in gold and ivory, as well as a frieze depicting battle scenes and processions of worshippers.

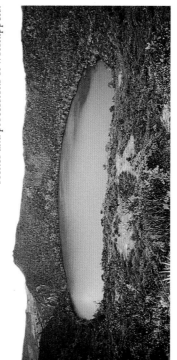

A human ancestor figure

GOLDEN WATERS

Gold was so important to the Peruvian Incas that they called it the sweat of the Sun god Inti. At El Dorado lake (above) in Colombia, each new king was coated in gold dust before sailing out to throw gold offerings into the water. The Spanish conquerors of Peru heard rumours of this, and searched in vain for the kingdom of El Dorado and its fabulous riches.

At sunrise and sunset, Uluru displays spectacular shades of orange and purple

MAJESTIC MOUNTAIN

The sacred site of Uluru, or Ayers Rock, rises from the central desert of Australia with great natural majesty. The focus of many myths among the Aborigines of central Australia, Uluru was said to have been built in the Dreamtime by two boys playing with mud after it rained.

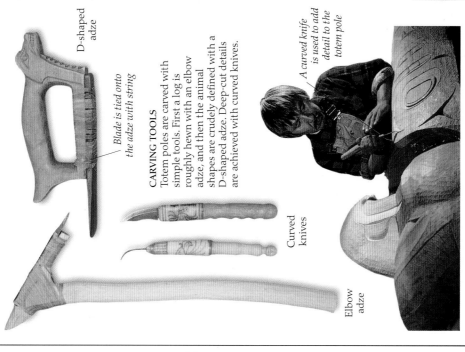

D-shaped adze

Blade is tied onto the adze with string

CARVING TOOLS

Totem poles are carved with simple tools. First a log is roughly hewn with an elbow adze, and then the animal shapes are crudely defined with a D-shaped adze. Deep-cut details are achieved with curved knives.

Curved knives

Elbow adze

A curved knife is used to add detail to the totem pole

WORKING THE WOOD

Totem poles are usually carved from red cedar, which grows up to 60 m (200 ft) tall. Carvers work up the pole from the bottom to the top, with the pole lying horizontally on its side. The wood is kept soft by dousing it with pans of hot water.

End of the world

JUST AS MYTHOLOGIES TELL how the world began, so they predict how it will end, often in a terrible fire or flood. The Aborigines of southeastern Australia believed that the end would come when one of the four props that held up the sky rotted away, allowing the sky to fall. The Native American Cherokee believed that the world was a great floating island, held by four cords hanging down from the sky, and that when these rotted through, the Earth would sink back beneath the sea. The ancient Egyptians, who feared every night that the Sun god Ra (pp.13, 44, 54) would be defeated in his journey through the underworld and fail to reappear, also foresaw a time when the god would grow so old and tired that he would forget who he was, so all he had created would come to an end.

The world will end when the rainbow serpent chews his own tail

COSMIC SERPENT
In west Africa Aido-Hwedo, the Rainbow Snake (pp.44, 50), carried the creator in his mouth while the world was made, and then circled around the Earth to hold it together. Red monkeys beneath the sea forge iron bars to feed him. When the iron runs out, Aido-Hwedo will chew his own tail, the world will convulse, and Earth and all its burdens will slide into the sea.

Rocky matter from an explosion in space

The world serpent has many heads

When Brahma awakes, he rises on a lotus flower from the god Vishnu

Lakshmi, Vishnu's wife, the goddess of fortune

At night, Vishnu rests on the world serpent, Shesha

END OF THE *KALPA*
For Hindus, time is an endless cycle of days and nights of Brahma (pp.6, 14), or *kalpas*. During the day, when Brahma is awake, the world is created anew. When Brahma goes to sleep, the *kalpa* ends. Each *kalpa* lasts 4,320 million years.

GREAT WORLD POLE

According to the Native American Cheyenne people, the Great White Grandfather Beaver of the North is gnawing the great pole that holds up the world. When he gnaws right through it, the world will end. The Tsimshian people of the northwest coast say that the pole on which the world spins is held up by Amala. He has a servant who gives him strength by rubbing his back with wild-duck oil once a year. The oil is nearly used up: when it runs out, Amala will die, and the world will fall.

North American family totem (symbol) of the beaver

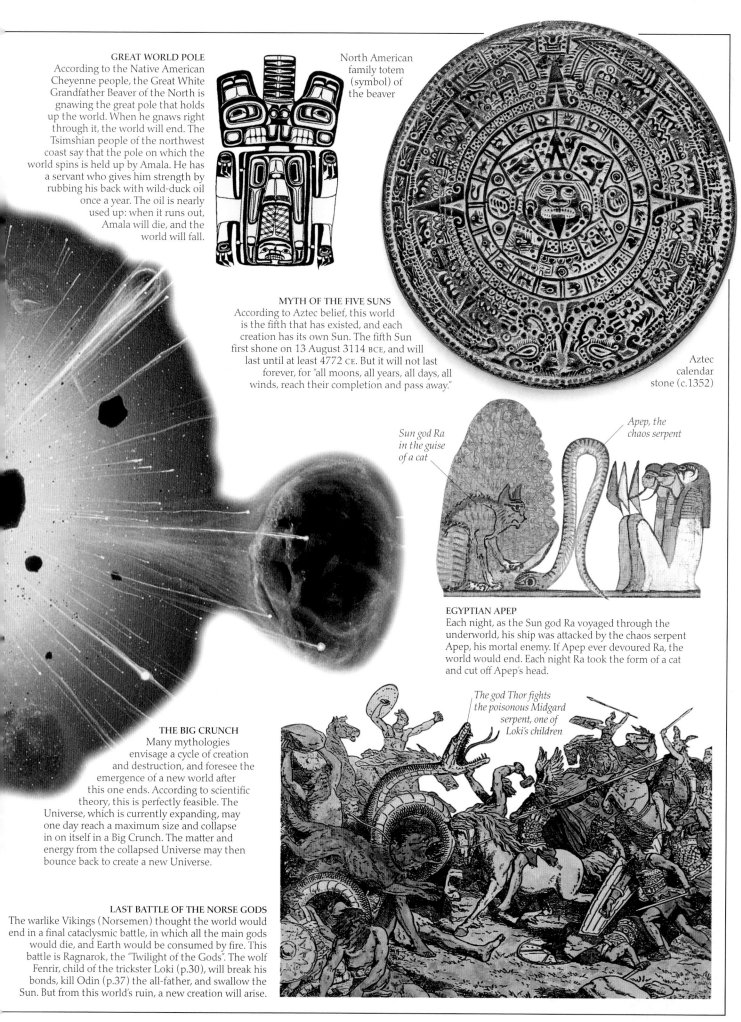

Aztec calendar stone (c.1352)

MYTH OF THE FIVE SUNS

According to Aztec belief, this world is the fifth that has existed, and each creation has its own Sun. The fifth Sun first shone on 13 August 3114 BCE, and will last until at least 4772 CE. But it will not last forever, for "all moons, all years, all days, all winds, reach their completion and pass away."

Sun god Ra in the guise of a cat

Apep, the chaos serpent

EGYPTIAN APEP

Each night, as the Sun god Ra voyaged through the underworld, his ship was attacked by the chaos serpent Apep, his mortal enemy. If Apep ever devoured Ra, the world would end. Each night Ra took the form of a cat and cut off Apep's head.

THE BIG CRUNCH

Many mythologies envisage a cycle of creation and destruction, and foresee the emergence of a new world after this one ends. According to scientific theory, this is perfectly feasible. The Universe, which is currently expanding, may one day reach a maximum size and collapse in on itself in a Big Crunch. The matter and energy from the collapsed Universe may then bounce back to create a new Universe.

The god Thor fights the poisonous Midgard serpent, one of Loki's children

LAST BATTLE OF THE NORSE GODS

The warlike Vikings (Norsemen) thought the world would end in a final cataclysmic battle, in which all the main gods would die, and Earth would be consumed by fire. This battle is Ragnarok, the "Twilight of the Gods". The wolf Fenrir, child of the trickster Loki (p.30), will break his bonds, kill Odin (p.37) the all-father, and swallow the Sun. But from this world's ruin, a new creation will arise.

Did you know?

MYTH AND FACT

The Sphinx was a mythical monster sent to punish the people of the Greek city of Thebes. She gobbled up anyone who could not solve her riddle: "What walks on four legs, two legs, and then three?" The answer was "man". He crawls on all fours as a baby, then walks upright on two legs, and has a third leg in old age – his walking stick!

The Canaanites of the Middle East had a grisly way of placating their thunder god, Baal. When they built a new house, a couple sacrificed a young child and buried it under the foundations.

Archaeologists have unearthed evidence to explain the trances of the Pythia – the priestess at Delphi, ancient Greece. Ethylene gas was escaping from faults in the rock, and this would have made the Pythia hallucinate. In her trance, she believed the god Apollo spoke to her.

According to an old Indian legend, the coastal town of Mahabalipuram in southern India once had seven beautiful temples – until the gods sent a flood to destroy the town. Today, only one temple stands on the seashore, but in 2002 divers found exciting evidence of six more temples under the sea.

The Giant's Causeway on the Antrim coast, Northern Ireland, is named after the giant Finn MacCool. According to legend, Finn built a causeway of huge stepping stones across the sea to Scotland. In reality, volcanic activity formed the hexagonal basalt stones about 60 million years ago.

In 2001, an archaeologist discovered the earliest known picture of the Mayan corn god. The mural, found in Guatemala, was painted around 100 CE. According to Mayan myth, the corn god went to the underworld but was later resurrected. Like the Greek story of Demeter, this myth would have explained the seasons and harvest.

One Greek myth tells how Leto (mother of Artemis and Apollo) turned some mean peasants into frogs. The peasants did not want her to drink from their lake, so they muddied the water with sticks. To punish them, Leto decided they would stay croaking in the mud forever.

A butterfly, symbol of the Pima creator god

The Pima Native Americans believed Great Butterfly, the creator god, flew down and made the first people from his own sweat. Across the Pacific, a tribe on the island of Sumatra, Indonesia, thought its ancestors had hatched from butterfly eggs.

One west African myth tells how the Earth mother, Iyadola, made the first people from clay. Some were white, because they were not fired enough. Some were fired too long and burned black. Others came out yellow, brown, or pink.

Leprechauns are creatures of Irish folklore. If caught by a human, they have to reveal the whereabouts of their hoard of gold.

Part of the Giant's Causeway in Antrim, Northern Ireland

There are many versions of the tale of how Arthur became king of the Britons. In one, Arthur proved his right to kingship by drawing Excalibur, an enchanted sword, from a stone. In another, the Lady of the Lake gave him the sword.

In Norse (Scandinavian) mythology, a terrible serpent was thought to lie coiled around the world at the bottom of the sea. Later, Norwegian sailors believed in the kraken, a many-armed sea monster that was 2.4 km (1.5 miles) across and capable of pulling a ship down into the ocean.

Mexican Tree of Life

Some modern Mexican artists create extraordinarily intricate images of the Tree of Life. They incorporate gods and other figures from Mayan and Aztec mythologies, mixed up with symbols borrowed from the Catholic Church.

On the Indonesian island of Java, *wayang kulit* (shadow puppet) plays enact traditional myths. Behind a cloth screen, the puppeteer operates the puppets with wires or rods. The audience sees the shadows projected onto the screen. Shows can last up to nine hours.

Javanese *wayang kulit*, made from leather

Tupan Patera crater on Jupiter's moon Io, photographed from the *Galileo* spacecraft

Q Do any of the planets have mythical associations?

A All of the planets in our Solar System, apart from Earth, are named after gods or goddesses. These are taken from the Roman pantheon (family of gods), with one exception – Uranos was the primordial sky god in Greek myth. The remaining six planets are named after Mercury, speedy messenger of the gods; Venus, goddess of love; Mars, god of farming and war; Jupiter, king of the gods; Saturn, god of the heavens; and Neptune, god of water.

Q Do any other landmarks in our Solar System have mythical names?

A Many of the moons are named after characters from myths. The Martian moons Phobos and Deimos, for example, take their names from two of the sons of Ares, the Greek god of war. Jupiter's four largest moons are called Ganymede, Callisto, Io, and Europa. These are all the names of characters from Greek myths whom Zeus kidnapped or seduced. Io, for example, was a beautiful nymph, but Zeus turned her into a cow to disguise her from his jealous wife Hera. Astronomers recently discovered a volcanic crater on Io, and that, too, has a mythical name – Tupan Patera, named after the Brazilian thunder god. It is about 75 km (47 miles) across and extremely active.

Temple of Kukulkan in Mexico

Q How does a Sami shaman drum up the spirit world?

A The Sami people live in northern Europe, across the countries of Finland, Norway, Sweden, and Russia. In some areas, they are still able to live as they have done for hundreds of years. Traditionally, each tribe has a shaman called a *noaide* who looks after the people's physical and spiritual health. He can also cast spells and tell prophecies. The shaman summons up the spirit world by entering a trance. To do this, he performs special rituals that include beating a magical drum called a *runebom*.

Q Which pyramid spoke in the voice of a god?

A Many experts agree that the Mayan Temple of Kukulkan at Chichen Itza, Mexico, produces echoes that sound like the cry of a quetzal bird – though not all are convinced the pyramid's acoustics were intentional. The quetzal was sacred to the Maya. It was linked to their god Kukulkan, the quetzal serpent – the same god as Quetzalcoatl, who was worshipped by the Aztecs. If a priest stood at the base of the temple steps and clapped, the pyramid answered in the divine quetzal's voice. The pyramid has another special effect. Around sunset at the spring and autumn equinoxes, a shadow resembling the quetzal serpent god seems to crawl down the staircase! Perhaps special ceremonies were held at the equinoxes, when Mayan worshippers could see the shadow and hear the echo at the same time.

Q Which animal links the Kongo world with the next world?

A The Kongo people live in central Africa. In traditional rituals, they use carved objects called *nkisi* to call up the spirits. *Nkisi* are hollow so they can be filled with magical herbs. One popular *nkisi* is Kozo, the dog. The Kongo believe dogs inhabit both the land of the living (the village) and the land of the dead (the forest where they hunt). The Kozo ritual figure usually has two heads, one to face each realm.

Kongo carving of Kozo (late 1800s)

Record breakers

§ OLDEST MYTHICAL PAINTINGS
Cave art found at Chauvet–Pont-d'Arc, France, dates back 31,000 years. It probably depicts important myths, and includes hundreds of animal figures.

§ OLDEST MYTHICAL STORY
Parts of the Babylonian *Epic of Gilgamesh* have been found on clay fragments dating from around 1700 BCE, but the story itself originated earlier – around 3000 BCE.

§ OLDEST ANCIENT WONDER
The Great Pyramid at Giza, Egypt, is the oldest survivor of the seven wonders of the ancient world. It was built around 4,500 years ago.

§ DIVINE STATUE
A statue of Vulcan, the Roman god of fire and volcanoes, cast for the 1904 World's Fair stood 15.25 m (50 ft) high.

Mythical meanings

Lotus flower

ELEMENTS FROM THE NATURAL WORLD often take on a symbolic meaning in myths and legends. They may have many different symbolisms in different cultures and mythologies. Here are just a few of the meanings attached to some plants, including flowers and fruits.

APPLE
The Norse (Scandinavian) gods ate the golden apples of Idun, goddess of spring, to stay young. There were golden apples in Greek mythology, too. The hero Heracles managed to steal them as one of his Twelve Labours, but first he had to kill Ladon, the 100-headed dragon that was guarding them.

ASH
Yggdrasil, the World Tree of Norse mythology, was a mighty ash. The Vikings (Norsemen) believed that the first people were carved from ash wood. In the Middle Ages, people sometimes fed babies on ash sap as it was thought to repel witches.

CHERRY
Cherries

The Chinese considered the cherry tree to be lucky and a symbol of spring. In Japan, samurai warriors used the cherry fruit as their emblem, perhaps because its blood-coloured flesh hid a tough, strong kernel.

DATE
In the deserts of north Africa and the Middle East, the date was always an important source of food and often linked with fertility. The ancient Egyptians associated the date palm with the Tree of Life, and pictures of date palms decorate their temples and shrines.

FIG
The Romans said their god of wine, Bacchus, created the fig. They also believed that their city's founders, Romulus and Remus, had been suckled under the shade of a fig tree on the banks of the River Tiber.

IRIS
The iris was the namesake of the Greek rainbow goddess. In Japanese folklore, irises protected homes from evil spirits.

IVY
The Greek god Dionysus was found under an ivy bush as a baby. He was often shown crowned with ivy and carrying an ivy-entwined staff. Ivy came to stand for longevity, perhaps because in nature ivy can carry on growing after its host tree has died.

Trailing ivy

JUJUBE TREE
The Taoists hold that the fruit of the jujube tree was the food of the gods. The tree's spiny branches were sometimes believed to have protective powers.

LAUREL
The laurel was linked to the Greek god Apollo. Daphne, the nymph he fell in love with, was turned into a laurel to escape him, and he wore a laurel leaf crown ever after. The Pythia at Delphi may have chewed laurel leaves during her trances in order to get closer to the god. Victorious Roman generals also wore laurel wreaths. In Chinese myth, the elixir of immortality was mixed beneath a laurel tree.

LILY
The lily was associated with the Greek goddess Hera – it was said to have sprung from her milk. Elsewhere it was a symbol of purity or prosperity.

Ancient Egyptian painting showing a date palm

LOTUS
Lotus flowers made up the crown of Osiris, the ancient Egyptian god of the underworld. The flower was an emblem of rebirth, because of the way it rose up from the muddy bed of the River Nile. The lotus is also key to the Hindu and Buddhist faiths as a symbol of Earth and creation.

MAIZE
The Aztecs worshipped several maize (corn) gods, and the plant was important to North American Indians, too, as a symbol of harvest and abundance. The Greeks and Romans worshipped their own corn goddesses – Demeter and Ceres.

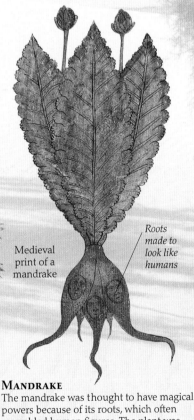

Medieval print of a mandrake

Roots made to look like humans

MANDRAKE
The mandrake was thought to have magical powers because of its roots, which often resembled human figures. The plant was said to scream when uprooted – and the sound was enough to kill a person! In Greek myth, the sorceress Circe used mandrake root in her spells.

MARIGOLD
The Chinese link this bright orange flower with the Sun and longevity. In India, it is the sacred flower of Krishna.

MUSHROOM

The Greeks associated the mushroom with ambrosia, the food of the gods. In European folklore, mushrooms and toadstools became associated with fairies and pixies, perhaps because of the way they spring up overnight, as if by magic.

Watercolour painting of a myrtle branch

MYRTLE

With its evergreen leaves and sweet scent, myrtle was linked with the Greek goddess of love, Aphrodite. It came to be a symbol of marital love and childbirth. In China, the plant was associated with success.

NARCISSUS

In Greek mythology, Narcissus was a beautiful youth who fell in love with his own reflection in a pool. Since he was unable to move from the pool's edge, he eventually wasted away. As a result, the narcissus flower is often seen as a symbol of early death. It was also the spring flower that Persephone was gathering when Hades whisked by in his chariot and carried her off to the underworld.

Narcissus flowers

OAK

The oak was important across Europe, representing might and longevity. In Greek mythology, Heracles's club was made of oak wood, and so was Jason's ship, the *Argo*. According to the Romans, the sky god Jupiter was sheltered under an oak as an infant. The Druids often held their sacred rites under oak trees.

OLIVE

Olives were very important to all the ancient civilizations around the Mediterranean, as a source of oil as well as food. In Greek legend, the goddess Athena was responsible for making the olive bear fruit. She did this when she was competing with the sea god, Poseidon, for control of Attica, the region around Athens. In Japan, the olive is a symbol of friendship and success.

PLUM

In China, the plum tree is associated with happy marriages and longevity, partly because it blooms so early. The great Chinese philosopher Lao-tse was said to have been born under a plum tree.

POMEGRANATE

The pomegranate is a symbol of fertility. While Persephone was in the underworld with Hades, she ate a pomegranate seed – this condemned her to spend four months of every year in the underworld.

Poppy

POPPY

Traditionally, the poppy was an emblem of sleep, death, and the soothing of pain, because of the properties of opium, which is found in poppies. More recently, the bright red of its petals has also made it a symbol of blood and slaughter.

ROSE

In Roman myth, the red rose sprang from the blood of the love goddess, Venus. She had caught her foot on the thorn of a white rose while running to the side of her dying lover Adonis. Venus's son Cupid used a rose to bribe the god of silence, when he wanted to put a stop to gossip about his mother.

ROSEMARY

The herb rosemary is known to have healing powers, but in European folklore it was used to protect against witches, fairies, evil spirits, and even storms. The Romans connected it to the goddess Venus.

Athena, ancient Greek goddess

TAMARISK

The tamarisk is a desert-growing tree that produces edible resin. In ancient Egypt, it was connected with the god Osiris. The Chinese held the tamarisk to be a symbol of immortality, and the Japanese associated it with life-giving rain.

VINE

The grapevine is the source of wine, and it was therefore linked with the Greek god Dionysus and the Roman god Bacchus. Followers of these gods drank wine to bring themselves in closer contact with the divine. Bunches of grapes often symbolized fruitfulness and plenty, but they could also suggest drunkenness.

WILLOW

The Ainu people of Japan said that a willow branch formed the spine of the first man. The Chinese connected willow with strength and flexibility.

YEW

The yew tree lives to a great age, so it appears mostly as a symbol of immortality. The Druids used to make their wands and bows out of yew wood. It was considered very unlucky to cut down a yew.

Find out more

Mʏᴛʜᴏʟᴏɢʏ ɪs ᴀʟʟ ᴀʀᴏᴜɴᴅ ʏᴏᴜ – so much so that sometimes you may not even notice it. Creatures of ancient myth pop up in modern stories, for example, and in many movies. You can also hunt out books or web pages that retell classical myths. In art galleries, you will see paintings that depict fascinating stories of gods and heroes. When you visit museums, look out for sacred artefacts or clothing that played a part in the storytelling of peoples from all over the world. You may even find that some of the festivals and traditions you observe are rooted in ancient myths.

AMPHITHEATRE ON THE ACROPOLIS, ATHENS, GREECE
Ancient Greek playwrights drew on their rich mythological heritage. Many of their works are still performed today in theatres around the world. One of the most amazing venues to see a Greek play, however, is in an ancient amphitheatre. The Odeon of Herodes Atticus was built around 161 CE. Performances are staged there each summer as part of the Athens Festival.

MYTHOLOGY AT THE MOVIES
Movie-makers often look to myths to find plots for their films. You may see *Jason and the Argonauts*, made in 1963, reshown on television. The film charts the quest of the Greek hero Jason for the Golden Fleece. Jason slays the dragon guarding the fleece and also faces many other dangers. He defeats harpies and tames fire-snorting bulls. He even manages to steer his ship through two moving cliffs that usually crushed anything that passed.

Jason's ship was the Argo, so his crew were known as the Argonauts

The sea god Poseidon

BRITISH MUSEUM, LONDON, UK
- Largest collection of Egyptian artefacts outside Cairo
- Mesoamerican treasures
- Prehistoric fertility figurines
- A Rapa Nui (Easter Island) statue
- Online access to the collections at www.britishmuseum.org/explore/highlights.aspx

CAMBRIDGE UNIVERSITY MUSEUM OF ARCHAEOLOGY AND ANTHROPOLOGY, CAMBRIDGE, UK
- Around 750,000 objects in total
- More than 30,000 Pacific artefacts
- 20th-century collection of British folklore

MUSÉE DE L'HOMME, PARIS, FRANCE
- Giant Rapa Nui (Easter Island) head statue
- Magical charms and amulets

MUSÉE DU LOUVRE, PARIS, FRANCE
- Numerous paintings of gods and monsters, such as Correggio's *Venus, Satyr, and Cupid*
- Antiquities from ancient Egypt, including exceptional figures of Bastet and Sekhmet
- Greek and Roman statuary, including the *Venus de Milo* (c.100 BCE)

MYTHSTORIES MUSEUM, WEM, SHROPSHIRE, UK
- The only UK museum dedicated exclusively to myths from around the world
- Interactive exhibits
- Extensive reference library

PITT RIVERS MUSEUM, OXFORD, UK
- Objects of magic, myth, and ritual, from prehistory to the present
- Amulets and costumes
- Artefacts are arranged by type, so it is easy to compare cultures

SMITHSONIAN INSTITUTION, WASHINGTON, DC, USA
- More than 140 million objects, artworks, and specimens
- Includes the National Museum of the American Indian and the National Museum of African Art

STANDING STONES AT CARNAC, FRANCE
Many ancient sacred sites can still be seen in the landscape. Visiting one of these sites is a good way to get closer to the people who created the earliest myths and stories. At Carnac, in southern Brittany, France, there are more than 3,000 stone monuments. They have been standing there for 6,000 years – since the Stone Age.

CORN DOLLY
Perhaps you have seen or even made a corn figure. Traditionally, this was made with the last sheaf of the harvest. It was kept safe because it contained the spirit of the corn.

BACCHUS AND ARIADNE (1521–1523)
If you are lucky enough to visit the National Gallery in London, UK, you may see this painting by Titian. It shows Bacchus, the Roman god of wine, when he first saw the princess Ariadne. He turned her crown into stars, so Titian painted stars twinkling in the sky above Ariadne's head.

HALLOWEEN SPOOKS
Halloween has its roots in Celtic rituals. The festival Samhain, held on 1 November, honoured the Celtic Lord of the Dead. The night before, he assembled all the wicked souls who had died in the past year.

BASTET THE CAT GODDESS
If you want to come face to face with an ancient god, visit a museum. This statue of the Egyptian goddess Bastet is on display in the Louvre, Paris, France. Many large museums have collections of objects that will help you find out more about ancient myths and the peoples who believed in them.

Glossary

ADZE An axe-like cutting tool.

AFTERLIFE A life after death.

AMULET A charm believed to have magical powers, and worn to bring good luck or ward off evil spirits.

ANCESTOR Someone from whom a person is descended.

ARCHAEOLOGIST Someone who studies artefacts made by humans long ago.

AVATAR The appearance of a Hindu god in physical form.

BIG BANG The huge explosion that created the Universe around 13,000 million years ago.

BODHISATTVA A Buddhist saint worthy of nirvana, who remains with humans in order to help them.

BOOMERANG A curved throwing weapon used by Australian Aborigines.

BREASTPLATE A piece of armour that protects the chest.

CATACLYSMIC Describes something that is – or causes – a total disaster.

CENTAUR A mythical creature, half man and half horse.

CHIMERA A mythical fire-breathing monster with three heads – a lion's, a goat's, and a serpent's.

Model of the Chimera

Krishna, an avatar (incarnation) of Vishnu

COSMOLOGY The study or explanation of order in the Universe.

COSMOS The whole world or Universe, seen to be arranged according to a particular pattern or order.

CULT A group of believers who are intensely devoted to one spiritual leader or divine figure.

CYCLOPS In Greek mythology, a one-eyed giant (plural: cyclopes).

DEITY A god or goddess.

DEMON A devil or evil spirit.

DISMEMBERED Describes a body that has been torn limb from limb.

DIVINE Describes a god.

DRAGON A mythical fire-breathing monster with a huge scaly body, wings, claws, and a tail. In Chinese myth, dragons are wingless, benevolent beings that live in water and the sky.

DREAMTIME The eternal present in which the sacred ancestors of the Australian Aborigines shaped human beings and the world. Aboriginal myths take place in the Dreamtime, which can be re-entered by ritual, song, and dance.

DRUID A Celtic priest.

ECSTASY A trance-like state of heightened joy.

ELIXIR A liquid possessing magical powers, such as granting immortality.

FERTILITY The ability to produce children or grow crops.

GORGON In Greek mythology, one of three monstrous, serpent-haired sisters – Stheno, Euryale, and Medusa.

GRIFFIN A mythical creature, half eagle, half lion.

HEADHUNTER A tribal warrior who collects the heads of his victims as trophies.

IMMORTAL Able to live forever; a being that will never die.

INCARNATION The appearance of a god in physical form.

INITIATED Accepted or admitted into a group – or a part of society – usually after going through certain important rites.

Painted lotus-shaped tiles from an ancient Egyptian temple

KALPA In Hindu cosmology, a period in which the Universe experiences one cycle of creation (when Brahma is awake) and destruction (when Brahma sleeps).

KATHAKALI A classical dance-drama from Kerala, southern India, usually performed by men and boys. Dancers mime to a sung story from a Hindu epic, such as the *Ramayana* or the *Mahabharata*.

KAYAK A sealskin canoe used by the Inuit.

LAVA Hot molten rock that erupts from a volcano or an opening in Earth's crust.

Map of Mesoamerica

LONGEVITY Living for a long time.

LOTUS A water lily growing in Egypt or India.

MACE A ceremonial staff or war club.

MERGED Joined or blended together.

MESOAMERICA An ancient region of Central America, comprising central and southern Mexico and the Yucatán Peninsula, Guatemala, Belize, El Salvador, western Honduras, and parts of Nicaragua and Costa Rica. Before the 16th-century Spanish conquest, Mesoamerica was home to civilizations such as the Aztecs and Maya.

MILKY WAY Our galaxy, a family of star systems held together by gravity, which contains our own Solar System.

MORTAL Destined to die; a being that will live for a limited time and then die.

MUMMIFIED Describes a body that has been turned into a mummy – that is, preserved so that it will not decay.

MYTH A story about gods or heroes that often explains how the world came to be as it is or how people should live in it. In everyday speech, the word "myth" is sometimes used to mean an untruth.

NEOLITHIC From the New Stone Age, which began around the time of the last ice age. Neolithic people used more complex stone tools than those of earlier ages, built stone structures, and began to make pottery.

NIRVANA The state of supreme happiness and enlightenment in Buddhism and Hinduism; an awareness of the true nature of human existence.

NORSE Scandinavian; in other words, from Sweden, Norway, or Denmark. Vikings were Norse people whose culture flourished between the 8th and 11th centuries CE.

NYMPH In Greek mythology, a beautiful young woman who usually had one divine parent. Nereids and oceanids were sea nymphs, naiads were water nymphs, oreads were mountain nymphs, and dryads were tree nymphs.

ORACLE A place where the words of a god are revealed, or the person through whom a god speaks.

PAGAN A person who follows a religion other than Christianity, Judaism, or Islam.

PEGASUS A mythical winged horse.

PHARAOH The title, meaning "great house", given to the kings of ancient Egypt. It originally referred to the royal palace, rather than the king.

PIGMENT The chemicals that give an object its colour. In their sacred sand-paintings, Native American Navajo use pigments made from plants and minerals.

PRIMORDIAL Existing at or from the very beginning of creation.

PROSPERITY Having good fortune, money, and success.

PYRAMID A stone structure with a square base and sloping sides. Pyramids could be royal tombs, as in Egypt, or sacrificial temples, as in Mesoamerica.

REINCARNATION The belief that a dead person is reborn in another body.

Aztec sacrificial knife

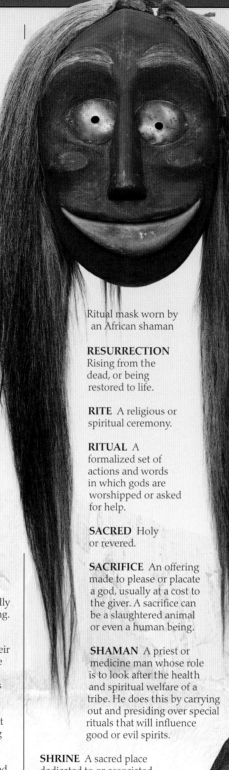

Ritual mask worn by an African shaman

RESURRECTION Rising from the dead, or being restored to life.

RITE A religious or spiritual ceremony.

RITUAL A formalized set of actions and words in which gods are worshipped or asked for help.

SACRED Holy or revered.

SACRIFICE An offering made to please or placate a god, usually at a cost to the giver. A sacrifice can be a slaughtered animal or even a human being.

SHAMAN A priest or medicine man whose role is to look after the health and spiritual welfare of a tribe. He does this by carrying out and presiding over special rituals that will influence good or evil spirits.

SHRINE A sacred place dedicated to or associated with a god, spirit, or holy object.

SOOTHSAYING Telling fortunes or predicting the future.

SORCEROR A wizard or magician who casts spells and has magical powers.

SPIRIT A bodiless person or being.

SUPERNATURAL Magical or spiritual and beyond the laws of nature.

TORII The entrance to a Shinto temple. Usually painted red, it consists of two vertical wooden posts, topped with two horizontal beams, of which the topmost extends beyond the supports.

TOTEM A Native American name for a spiritual ancestor. A totem can be a living creature, for example an eagle, or an inanimate object, such as a river.

TRIBE A group of people who are often related and share the same language and culture.

TRICKSTER A person or god who plays tricks or deceives.

TSUNAMI A huge sea wave, usually triggered by a volcano or earthquake.

UNDERWORLD A mythical region below Earth where people are said to live after death.

UNICORN A mythical horse with a spiral horn on its forehead.

VALHALLA In Norse (Scandinavian) mythology, the great hall of Odin, where dead heroes feast and fight in the afterlife.

VALKYRIE In Norse (Scandinavian) mythology, one of the female battle spirits who guide heroes to Valhalla.

VISION A mystical or religious experience in which a person sees a god or spirit.

YANG In Chinese philosophy, one of the two complementary principles (the other is yin). Yang is positive, active, bright, warm, and masculine.

YIN In Chinese philosophy, one of the two complementary principles (the other is yang). Yin is negative, passive, dark, cold, and feminine.

Ornate Viking stone from the Swedish island of Gotland, showing a Norse warrior riding into Valhalla

Stonehenge, in Wiltshire, UK, was built over a period of 1,500 years from 3100 BCE. It may have been part of a larger sacred landscape, marking the end of a ritual procession from Woodhenge, 3 km (2 miles) northeast, that symbolically enacted the journey from life to death.

The Greek gods lived beyond a gate of clouds above the peak of Mount Olympus. In this ceiling painting of 1528 by Giulio Romano, Zeus, the king of the gods, can be seen brandishing his thunderbolt (bottom centre).

Index

Acknowledgements

Dorling Kindersley would like to thank: Akan Hills, Philip Nicholls, Christi Graham, John Williams, Kevin Lovelock, Jim Rossiter, and Janet Peckham of the British Museum, London; Kalamandalam Vijayakumar and Kalamandalam Barbara Vijayakumar; and the African Crafts Centre, Covent Garden, London.
Photography: Andy Crawford
Researcher: Robert Graham
Index: Chris Bernstein
Design assistance: Jill Bunyan and Anna Martin
Proofreading: Sarah Owens
Wallchart: Peter Radcliffe, Steve Setford
Clipart CD: Jo Little, Claire Watts, Jessamy Wood

Picture credits:
The Publishers would like to thank the following for their kind permission to reproduce their photographs:

(Key: a-above; b-below/bottom; c-centre; f-far; l-left; r-right; t-top)

AKG Images: 37tr, 37l; Boymans van Beuningen Museum, Rotterdam *The Tower of Babel*, Pieter Brueghel the Elder 7r; Erich Lessing/Württembergisches Landesmuseum, Stuttgart 7bcr, 24tl, 44tl; SMPK Kupferstichkabinett, Berlin 12tl; Torquil Cramer 56/57c; Universitets Oldsaksamling, Oslo 32bc; Von der Heydt Museum, Wuppertal *Flora, Awakening Flowers*, 1876, by Arnold Bucklin (1827–1901) 23bl; **American Museum of Natural History:** 41br, 48tr, 50cl; Thos. Beiswenger 39r; **Ancient Art & Architecture Collection:** 58tl; D.F. Head 29tr; Ronald Sheridan 8bl, 11br, 21d, 24br, 25ar, 43l, 43ca; **The Art Archive:** Buonconsiglio Castle Trento/Dagli Orti 60cr; Musée du Louvre Paris/Dagli Orti 63br; National Gallery London/Eileen Tweedy 63c; Dagli Orti 59bc, 60bc; Mireille Vautier 58bl; **Ashmolean Museum, Oxford:** 14c, 30br, 40/41c; **Duncan Baird Publishers Archive:** 14tl; Japanese Gallery 9cr, 31c; **Bildarchiv Preußischer**

Kulturbesitz: 32tl; SMPK Berlin 16; Staatliche Museum, Berlin 46tr; **Bridgeman Art Library, London/New York:** British Museum, London *The Weighing of the Heart Against Maat's Feather of Truth*, Egyptian, early 19th Dynasty, c.1300 BCE, *Book of the Dead of the Royal Scribe* 52br; By Courtesy of the Board of the Trustees of the V&A *Vishnu in the Centre of his Ten Avatars*, Jaipur area, 18th century 18tl; Galleria degli Uffizi, Florence, Italy *The Birth of Venus*, c.1485, by Sandro Botticelli (1444/5–1510) 40cl; Louvre, Paris, France/Giraudon *Stele of a Woman before Re- Harakhy*, Egyptian, c.1000BC 13tl; Musée Condé, Chantilly, France MS 860/401 f.7 *The Story of Adam and Eve*, detail from "Cas des Nobles Hommes et Femmes" by Boccaccio, translated by Laurent de Premierfait, French 1465, *Works of Giovanni Boccaccio* (1313–75) 7bl (right), 15br; Museo Correr, Venice, Italy *Glimpse of Hell* (panel) by Flemish School (15th century) 53bl; Palazzo del Te, Mantua, Italy, *The Gods of Olympus*, trompe l'oeil ceiling from the Sala dei Giganti, 1528 (fresco), Romano, Giulio (1492–1546) (workshop of) 68–69; Piazza della Signoria, Florence/Lauros – Giraudon *Perseus with the Head of a Medusa*, 1545–1554, in the Loggia dei Lanzi, by Benvenuto Cellini (1500–1571) 33bcr; Private Collection Genesis 6:11–24 Noah's Ark, Nuremberg Bible (Biblia Sacra Germanaica), 1483 19cb; **British Museum:** 4br, 4bl, 7bc, 11tr, 12tr, 14r, 15c, 15r, 15r, 15tr, 17r, 21t, 23tl, 26bl, 29br, 33 tr, 34c, 36br, 37bc, 40tl, 41tc, 41tr, 50bl, 51tl; **Cambridge Museum of Anthropology:** 19r, 55tr; **Central Art Archives:** The Old Students House, Helsinki 17tl; **Jean-Loup Charmet:** 7tr, 19tl; **Christie's Images:** *In the Well of the Great Wave of Kanagawa*, c.1797, by Hokusai Katsushika (1760–1849) 18/19b, 28r, 29l; **Bruce Coleman Ltd:** Jeff Foott Productions 42tl; **Corbis:** 66–67; Chinch Gryniewicz/Ecoscene 60–61; Michael S. Yamashita 62–63; **CM Dixon:** 29bc; **DK Picture Library:** American Museum of Natural History/ Lynton Gardiner 65tc; British Museum

64tr; Glasgow Museum 64tcl; INAH/ Michel Zabé 65bl; Statens Historika Museum, Stockholm 65br; **Edimedia:** 12cr; **E.T. Archive:** 31l; British Library Or 13805 54bl; Freer Gallery of Art 22br; Victoria & Albert Museum, London 10/11c; **Mary Evans Picture Library:** 10bl, 10br, 21bl, 26c, 28tl, 30bl; **Werner Forman Archive:** Anthropology Museum, Veracruz University, Jalapa 53r; Arhus Kunstmuseum, Denmark 30cl; Dallas Museum of Art 26bl; David Bernstein Fine Art, New York 49r; Field Museum of Natural History, Chicago 9t; Museum of the American Indian, Heye Foundation 13cl; Smithsonian Institution 12bl; State Museum of Berlin 16cl; **Glasgow Museums (St Mungo):** 31bl, 32bl, 38bl, 48br, 52tr; **Ronald Grant Archive:** Columbia Pictures 62bc; **Hamburgisches Museum für Völkerkunde:** 43tr; **Robert Harding Picture Library:** Patrick Mathews 52bl; **Heritage Image Partnership:** James Sowerby 61cla; **Michael Holford:** British Museum 7cr (below), 8bc, 8tl, 13bl, 14bl, 40bl, 55cr; Kunisada 13br; Museum of Mankind 42bl; Victoria & Albert Museum, London 9br; **Hutchison Library:** Ian Lloyd 57br; **Images Colour Library:** 24c, 55br, 56tr; **Impact:** Mark Henley 57tr; **INAH/Michael Zabe:** 19tc, 22l, 16bc; **Barnabas Kindersley:** 53tl, 53ca; **Lonely Planet Images:** George Tsafos 62tr; **MacQuitty International Photo Collection:** 39bl; **Nilesh Mistry:** 30tl; **Musée de L'Homme, France:** 20l; D Ponsard 36l, 54tl; **Museum of Anthropology, Vancouver:** 57cl; **Museum of Mankind:** 4cl, 32c, 35tc; **NASA:** 59tl; **National Maritime Museum:** 2c, 47tr; **National Museum of Copenhagen:** 34/35b; **The Board of Trustees of the National Museums & Galleries on Merseyside:** 28bl, 51tr; **Natural History Museum, London:** 2tcl, 27tr, 27c, 46/47b, 46tl, 47tl, 47r, 64bl; © David Neel, 1998: 2tl; **Peter Newark's Pictures:** 6br, 16r, 39cl, 49c; **Panos Pictures:** Caroline Penn 57bl; **Ann & Bury Peerless:** 20cl, 45tl; **Pitt Rivers Museum, Oxford:** 6bcl, 10tr, 23cr, 38tr 51bl; Zither 17c; **Planet Earth Pictures:** Jan Tove Johansson 8l;

Axel Poignant Archive: 11cl, 21br, 35tl; **Rex Features:** Tim Brooke 53bcl; **Rijksmuseum voor Volkenkunde:** 20r; **Réunion des Musées Nationaux Agence Photographique:** Hervé Lewandowski 26tl, 33cr; Richard Lambert 37cbr; **Royal Ontario Museum:** 61tr; **Science Photo Library:** Chris Bjornberg 8/9c; Sally Benusen (1982) 54/55c; **South American Pictures:** Tony Morrison 13tr, 57cr; **Spectrum Colour Library:** 56cr; **Statens Historika Museum, Stockholm:** 7br; **Oliver Strewe:** 50cr; 29cra; **Topham Picturepoint:** 58cr, 59cra, 63tl.

Wallchart:
Alamy Images: Ancient Art & Architecture Collection Ltd cra (ishtar); Image Gap bl; **Dorling Kindersley:** Courtesy of The American Museum of Natural History cl (Shaman mask); Courtesy of the Manchester Museum clb (Apphrodite); Courtesy of the National Museum, New Delhi cr (Durga); Courtesy of the Royal Ontario Museum, Toronto tl; Courtesy of the University Museum of Archaeology and Anthropology, Cambridge fbr; James McConnachie / Rough Guides bc (Chimera); Rob Reichenfeld / Courtesy of Bishop's Museum, Hawaii crb (Ku War God); **Getty Images:** Guy Edwardes / Photographer's Choice ftl; Robert Harding br (Dogon); Jeremy Woodhouse / Photodisc crb (coyote); **Photolibrary:** Brand X Pictures fbr (skull).

Jacket:
Front: **Dorling Kindersley:** The British Museum ftr; St Mungo, Glasgow City Council Museums c. **Edimedia:** tr. **Ann & Bury Peerless:** tc. *Back:* **Ancient Art & Architecture Collection:** Ronald Sheridan cb. **Christie's Images Ltd:** l. **Dorling Kindersley:** The American Museum of Natural History fcra; Ashmolean Museum cla; The British Museum cr, cra; **The Natural History Museum, London:** Kokoro br.

All other images © Dorling Kindersley. For further information see: www.dkimages.com